The Narcissist in Your Life

5 Steps to Identifying and Healing Yourself from Toxic and Narcissistic Relationships

Max J. Harrison

© Copyright 2019 - All rights reserved.

The content contained within this book may not be reproduced, duplicated or transmitted without direct written permission from the author or the publisher.

Under no circumstances will any blame or legal responsibility be held against the publisher, or author, for any damages, reparation, or monetary loss due to the information contained within this book. Either directly or indirectly.

Legal Notice:

This book is copyright protected. This book is only for personal use. You cannot amend, distribute, sell, use, quote or paraphrase any part, or the content within this book, without the consent of the author or publisher.

Disclaimer Notice:

Please note the information contained within this document is for educational and entertainment purposes only. All effort has been executed to present accurate, up to date, and reliable, complete information. No warranties of any kind are declared or implied. Readers acknowledge that the author is not engaging in the rendering of legal, financial, medical or professional advice. The content within this book has been derived from various sources. Please consult a licensed professional before attempting any techniques outlined in this book.

By reading this document, the reader agrees that under no circumstances is the author responsible for any losses, direct or indirect, which are incurred as a result of the use of information contained within this document, including, but not limited to, — errors, omissions, or inaccuracies.

Table Of Contents

Table Of Contents 5

Introduction 9

  Narcissism in Today's World 12

Step 1: Understand the Concept of Narcissism 14

  Origin of the Concept of Narcissism 15

  The 3 Major Types of Narcissism and the 5 Subtypes 16
    Classic Narcissism 17
    Malignant Narcissism 22
    Vulnerable Narcissism 26
    Cerebral Narcissism vs. Somatic Narcissism 31
    Overt Narcissism vs. Covert Narcissism 35
    Inverted Narcissism 39

  Narcissistic Personality Disorder (NPD) 41
    What Is the Difference between Narcissism and Narcissistic Personality Disorder? 41
    What Are the Causes of Narcissistic Personality Disorder? 42
    What Are the Symptoms of Narcissistic Personality Disorder? 46
    What Are the Consequences of Narcissistic Personality Disorder? 49
    Can Narcissistic Personality Disorder Be Clinically Diagnosed? 52

Can You Grow out of Narcissistic Personality Disorder? 53

Step 1: A Summary 55

Step 2: Assess if You Have Narcissistic Personality Disorder 57

Questions to Ask Yourself 58
A Test Approved by Professionals 60

Which Steps Should I Take if I Have NPD? 60

How Can I Change the Narcissistic Patterns in My Life? 65

Step 2: A Summary 67

Step 3: Assess Who Is the Narcissist in Your Life 69

Narcissism in Your Relationship 70
What Are the Warnings Signs to Look Out For? 76
The Concept of Codependency 80
A Narcissist "Love" Story: An Example 82

Narcissism in Your Family 85
Narcissistic Parents 85
Narcissistic Siblings 95
Narcissistic Kids 98

Narcissism in Your Friendships 99
Signs Your Friend Is Narcissistic 100
A Narcissistic Friendship: An Example 103

Narcissism at Work 105
Signs Your Colleague Is Narcissistic 106

Signs Your Boss Is Narcissistic 111

Step 3: A Summary 117

Step 4: Understand Common Triggers of NPD 121

Is Aging a Trigger to the Worsening of NPD? . 125

How to Deal with Your Triggers 127

Step 4: A Summary 137

Step 5: Understand How You Can Deal with the Narcissist in Your Life 139

How Can I Deal with My Narcissist Partner? ..140
When Your Partner Is Abusive.. 140
When Your Partner Wants to Change................................147
Dealing with a Narcissistic Partner: Michael and Stephanie's Story.. 151

Tips to Deal with a Narcissist Family Member 153
With Your Narcissistic Parent...153
With Your Narcissistic Sibling 157
Parenting a Narcissistic Child...159

Tips to Deal with a Narcissist Friend 160
Dealing with a Narcissistic Friend: Paul's Example.......... 161

Tips to Deal with a Narcissist at Work............ 162
If It Is Your Coworker 162
If It Is Your Boss.. 164

Step 5: A Summary.. 167

Conclusion 169

Resources *172*

Introduction

Narcissism is defined as an exaggerated sense of self-importance that results in traits such as lack of interest in others, a sense of entitlement, and selfishness. In some cases, it is so extreme that it turns into a mental condition that has deep consequences on the person's well-being and relationships with others. This mental condition is called narcissistic personality disorder (NPD).

In this book, I will get into more detail about the concepts of narcissism and narcissistic personality disorder and help you understand these concepts. More importantly, this book is a step-by-step guide for you to figure out if someone around you is narcissistic. You will learn how that affects your life and how you can deal with it.

There are five steps to this book. In each one, I will explain the concepts and warning. I will also give you suggestions and practical examples. (It is important to note that all names and stories are fictitious unless stated otherwise and that the gender used for each example is chosen at random as narcissism exists on people from every gender identity). If you recognize yourself in any situation, you might have a narcissistic person around you, and it is important to know how not to let that person negatively affect you.

By the end of this book, my hope is that you have a better understanding of NPD and know whether it exists in your life. Also, you should be able to recognize any consequent situations where you should remove yourself from.

However, before we dive into it all, I would like you to consider narcissism as a trait that you and the people you deal with in your life possess. Aren't we all a little bit narcissistic? Maybe it's not to the point where it has major negative consequences, but if we consider the possibility that narcissism is a spectrum that goes from "healthy narcissism" to "harmful narcissism," we all fit in some part of it. Following this logic, you can say that narcissism is not always a bad thing. If you are on the healthier side of the spectrum, it is actually helpful for you as it allows you to have an evened sense of self-worth and respect for yourself, therefore helping you navigate through life with due consideration both for yourself and for those around you. In fact, healthy narcissism is needed for anyone who wants to achieve goals for themselves. However, the further you get from that side of the spectrum, the more detrimental narcissism can be for you, and that is where an intervention is needed as we will see throughout this book.

Narcissism in Today's World

It is commonly said that there are more narcissists now than ever, with some even referring to it as an epidemic. Social media is often said to be the reason why this is such a rising trend, and it is quite easy to understand why. We post every single day about our lives. We take selfies and record each moment just to show it to the world, and we hope that we will get x amount of likes. Otherwise, we might even delete those posts. Furthermore, we follow and worship other people who do the same, encouraging this cycle of narcissism. It is an easy way of getting and giving attention, and that can get into some people's heads, especially those with low self-esteem and a constant need of attention (which is also the case with narcissists as we will see further in the book).

Some may say that posting photos and videos of good moments in life can be seen as a form of celebration, which is also valid. As mentioned before, being on the healthy side of the narcissistic spectrum can be a good thing, and praising yourself with a selfie is definitely not something bad. However, when it is taken to the extreme, it can have severe consequences.

A study conducted by *The Open Psychology Journal* showed that posting a lot of photos (particularly selfies) is directly correlated to the development of narcissistic traits ("Visual Social Media Use Moderates the Relationship between Initial Problematic Internet Use and Later Narcissism," 2019). During four months, 74 university students and their internet usage were observed. They took the narcissism personality inventory and the problematic internet use questionnaire. After those four months, it was concluded that those who used the internet for visual purposes (that is, for posting photos and videos) showed traits of narcissism while those who mainly conducted verbal usage of the internet did not.

The growth of narcissism and its correlation to social media can become very harmful not only mentally but also physically, with people putting themselves in dangerous situations just from the Gram. This is why it becomes essential to be able to recognize the traits of a narcissist and know how to deal with one.

Step 1: Understand the Concept of Narcissism

If we put it simply, narcissists are those with a magnified sense of self. They see themselves as superior and worthy of more, and they need to be the center of attention all the time. They look at others with a lack of empathy or interest, which damages relationships and other people's well-being (as well as their own).

However, the reason for this type of behavior is more often than not connected to a complete contrary sense of self. Deep down, they have very low self-esteem and use the narcissism as a mask. They hide behind selfish thoughts and behaviors because they don't want to be real and because admitting to their flaws and weaknesses means putting themselves in a vulnerable situation in front of others, which is something they continuously run away from. Narcissism is a concept that is deeper than it may seem to a lot of people as there is a lot more to it than a simple sense of supremacy.

Origin of the Concept of Narcissism

Metamorphoses is a poem written by Ovid, a Roman poet who died in the year 17 BC. Ovid wrote countless poems that have since then been studied and published. In *Metamorphoses*, Ovid tells the story of a beautiful young man called Narcissus, a character of the Greek mythology, who has several women interested in him and who has never seen his own image, so is only be aware of how he looks by the reactions of others. Echo, a nymph, ends up falling in love with Narcissus, but the love is not reciprocated, and that causes Echo to die. After that, one of Echo's handmaidens prays to the goddess of revenge, Nemesis, and the goddess punishes Narcissus by declaring that if he ever falls in love, his feelings will never be reciprocated.

One day, Narcissus finally sees his own reflection in a pool of water in the forest that he was drinking from and ends up falling deeply in love with it. He tries to kiss his image, but every time he does so, it disintegrates as the water dissolves. And just like Echo, he dies from unreturned love.

This is the story that originated the concept of narcissism. In it, the main character could not recognize his own reflection, and he did not consider the feelings of those who had fallen in love with him. In other words, there was no self-awareness or sympathy for others.

When Ovid wrote this story, he did not intend to start this new concept; but years later, in 1898, Havelock Ellis, an English essayist, psychologist, and physician who specialized in the study of human sexual behavior, used the term "Narcissus-like" in his article "Autoerotism: A Psychological Study" to describe someone who sees themselves as their own sexual object.

After Ellis, others such as Freud and Ernest Jones used Narcissus as a term of comparison, and over time, the concept of narcissism was established.

The 3 Major Types of Narcissism and the 5 Subtypes

We have mentioned before that narcissism is a spectrum. There is no unique pattern to how it comes up in one's actions, and as such, it is possible (and convenient) to categorize narcissists into different types and subtypes according to the traits they present, the behaviors they have, and what leads to their narcissism.

There are three main types on narcissists: the classic, the malignant, and the vulnerable. From those, five other subcategories were created: cerebral, somatic, overt, covert, and inverted. Being able to recognize which type of narcissist you have in your life can make it a lot easier for you to know how you can deal with them and have a better grasp of why they act the way they do.

Classic Narcissism

As the name suggests, a classic narcissist is probably the one you imagined when you first read the word "narcissist" in this book. You can tell who classic narcissists are from a mile away—the people who need everyone's attention on themselves and who clearly behave as if they were better than those around them. Although they are easy to recognize, we mostly see them as "annoying" and not as people who may have a severe self-esteem problem as is the case a lot of the times. This is because they function just like anyone would (hence the fact that they are often referred to as high-functioning narcissists), except with what seems to be a bit of an attitude. Those around this type of person might not be big fans of such an attitude, but they also do not see it as more than that.

Common Traits of a Classic Narcissist

- They have an inflated sense of self.

- They get angry when people don't treat them like the superior person they consider themselves to be.

- They are often assertive, arrogant, and extravagant.

- They are not able to recognize their own mistakes and learn from them.

- They lack regard for other people's feelings.

- They would rather do something that would only benefit themselves as opposed to something that would benefit the group.

- They don't feel that they need to follow the rules.

- They like to dominate.

- They are not good listeners, particularly when faced with criticism. In those situations, they often choose to ignore it instead of using the feedback to better themselves.

- They like to speak, but they do not like to teach. Bragging about their knowledge is preferred to sharing it.

- They are very competitive.

An Example of a Classic Narcissist

To exemplify the behavior of a classic narcissist, all we need to do is think of someone who has been in a globally known position of leadership. Whoever just came up in your mind is possibly a classic narcissist. Of course, there are great leaders in the world—people who fight for the greater good and lead with honesty and empathy for everyone despite any hierarchical differences. However, we all know that that is not always the case.

A classic narcissist has all the traits someone needs to lead a group while making sure that they end up being the person benefiting the most during their leadership. They are great at gaining followers through their compelling communication skills. They speak with confidence and know how to make an audience excited about something even if it does not truly mean much of an improvement to the quality of their lives. They have a need for other people's praise, and because they are superior to others (in their mind), they are the best choice to fill in a position of authority. And the more praise they get, the more dangerous their leadership becomes because to them it feels like a confirmation of their superiority.

Anyone who tries to go against a classic narcissist gets ignored. They don't need your help or advice because you are less than them, and if you don't agree with them, it is your loss. They do this because, deep down, they are afraid to get in touch with their emotions and they cannot take criticism in a positive way. They build a wall around them, and they don't let in anyone who might be a threat to this grandiose image they have built in their audience's eyes. Criticism, even if constructive, is always seen as an attack, and not listening is the defense mechanism of choice for classic narcissists.

Someone in a position of authority who is often referred to as a narcissist leader is Elon Musk, the CEO of Tesla. In 2018, Musk found himself in several negative instances that created headlines, namely the fatality caused by a navigation mistake on a Tesla autopilot and the discovery of work injuries that he was trying to hide in order to prove that his factory was a safer place for his employees. These would be tough situations for anyone to deal with, let alone someone who is in the public eye.

However, if you look at Musk's responses to these and other events, you can clearly recognize the traits of narcissism in his personality. Never did he take responsibility for what happened; instead, he lied to his audience and did what he could to avoid rules and punishments.

Classic narcissists are not just in top positions; they are also around us, common human beings. Let's take the example of Joshua, who is a recruiter at a tech company. He is part of a team of five, led by his boss, Sarah. Joshua is good at his job. He always speaks confidently and with enthusiasm to his prospects and is often able to attract talent to the company.

However, Joshua does not always play by the book. Through his great communication skills, he manages to get the most interviews out of the team even if that means "stealing" his fellow recruiters' prospects instead of working toward a balanced teamwork environment. Whenever Sarah tries to speak to him about why rules and company guidelines exist and make him understand that he needs to follow them just like his colleagues do in order to work as a team and divide efforts to achieve the goals more efficiently, he chooses to ignore her. After all, he sees himself as better than Sarah, so it does not even make sense to him that she is in a higher position in the company hierarchy.

Joshua is not a team player. He puts himself before the team and the company. He does not believe that the rules apply to him, and he cannot take his boss's criticism in order to improve his performance at work. Joshua is a classic narcissist.

Malignant Narcissism

Malignant narcissists, or toxic narcissists, can be a scary type of people to deal with. It is like the ultimate level or narcissism, where the severity of all the symptoms and traits is multiplied, making these individuals a threat to themselves and to others. Because the symptoms are so intense, helping these people to overcome their narcissism is an extremely difficult task.

Even just having narcissists of the toxic type in one's life can be difficult, mostly because you can never be sure of how they will react to what happens around and to them. When they feel threatened (which is often, since their self-esteem is so low), they can react impulsively and be aggressive toward others. And there is also a sadistic side to malignant narcissism because they enjoy having those impulsive and aggressive reactions. Causing pain and humiliation is something that brings them satisfaction, and to them, there is a thrill that comes with ruining other people's lives. This explains why a lot of them maintain relationships of abuse with others and end up becoming remorseless criminals.

This type of narcissism is actually a combination of two personality disorders—narcissistic personality disorder and antisocial personality disorder. The first one is like narcissism 2.0, where it is more than just a group of traits that the person presents, and it becomes a mental disorder. The second one, on the other hand, is characterized by impulsive, aggressive, reckless, and ruthless behavior. This mix is the perfect recipe to create such a complicated and impulsive psyche.

The term "malignant narcissism" actually originated from one of the scariest group of people that ever took part in the history of the world—the Nazis. It was based on their behavior that Erich Fromm, a globally known German psychoanalyst who escaped from Nazi Germany before World War II, created the concept in

1964. Fromm characterized malignant narcissists as the "quintessence of evil" (Zeiders, 2016).

Common Traits of a Malignant Narcissist

- Out of all the types and subtypes, they show the harshest traits of narcissism.

- They are usually antisocial.

- They lie often.

- They are aggressive and sometimes even sadistic.

- They show symptoms similar to sociopaths and psychopaths.

- They are paranoiac.

- They are very resistant to change or improvements.

- They take any chance they can to humiliate others.

- They believe that if they say something, it is automatically true.

- They are jealous of other people's victories.

- They are superficial and don't give proper value to their relationships.

- They see everything in black and white.

- They use mind games to control the victims of their abuse.

An Example of a Malignant Narcissist

Once again, we can look at some globally known leaders to illustrate cases of malignant narcissism. These are the leaders who caused pain to their community and adopted harmful behaviors that even cost other people's lives. They are the epitome of narcissism and caused huge pain with no remorse. Now that you know the origin of the concept, you can probably guess who was one of the most infamous malignant narcissists in history—Hitler. Like him, there were others, such as Stalin and Mussolini. And now, in 2019, Donald Trump is considered by many to be one of the latest of additions to the group of malignant narcissistic world leaders because of the values and beliefs he shares and the decisions and actions he has taken thus far.

Malignant narcissism doesn't just exist in the form of genocide or mass discrimination; it also exists at a smaller scale as you will see with the example of Laura, a young woman who has always kept to herself and has never been close to almost anyone. Ever since Laura was a child, scenes of extreme violence never caused much of a reaction, and once, after she saw a kid in a movie purposely kill a frog, she decided to try it in real life. Years went by, and Laura met Steve, for whom she created a growing interest. In order to get that interest to be mutual, Laura lied to him about her personality, and after a while, they got together.

After years of being in a relationship, Laura started showing her true colors and slowly shifted back to her antisocial, aggressive, impulsive being. With this came instances of verbal and physical abuse toward Steve, followed by the use of manipulation techniques for him not to leave her. Anytime Steve tries to go against her, Laura tries to hurt him physically, and when he threatens that he will break up with her, she says she will kill herself. Laura is a liar, an abuser, and a master manipulator. She has zero regards for Steve's feelings and safety. She is a malignant narcissist.

Vulnerable Narcissism

Just like the others, vulnerable narcissists see themselves as superior. However, what sets them apart is that they don't like to be the center of attention, and they are in touch with their emotions, which might make them harder to recognize. You might even know one or two narcissists of this type, and you don't even suspect it.

Vulnerable narcissists use self-centeredness as a mask, but they can be quick to turn into a completely different person who actually feels and acts inferior to others and can adopt problematic behaviors. All they need in order to make this shift is the slightest feeling that they are being threatened. This threat can be real if someone confronts them about something, for example, or simply in their mind if they overthink about something someone has said and create problems where they actually do not exist.

These people go from believing that they are more than others and they deserve better than others to experiencing extreme feelings of anxiety, worthlessness, panic attacks, and depression. Psychologically, they are awfully unbalanced. In the eyes of a vulnerable narcissist, they are always a victim, and everyone around them is out to get them. They don't understand how not everyone sees how perfect they really are and acts accordingly.

Similar to malignant narcissism, vulnerable narcissism

is also linked to a mental condition, and that is depression. This is a common illness on narcissists of this type because the life they have and the life they believe they deserve don't match. They are also sometimes compared to people with a bipolar personality disorder because of the constant shifts between feeling on top of the world and feeling anxious and unhappy.

Common Traits of a Vulnerable Narcissist

- They are very sensitive and victimize themselves often.

- Emotionally, they demand a lot from those around them, which becomes extremely exhausting for anyone who knows them.

- They are passive-aggressive.

- At first sight, it might seem like they are just introverted people. They have unrealistically high expectations from the people they meet, and when those expectations aren't met, they simply give up on people and they isolate themselves. However, over time, you start noticing slight narcissistic traits that someone who is just an introvert would not show.

- They have a lot of mood swings.

- They often threaten to hurt themselves in order to finish and win a conflict (and most of them don't actually follow through with the threat).

- They tend to take offense at other people's emotions even if these are not related to them.

- They blame others for their own mistakes.

- They give fake apologies a lot.

- They are often judgmental people who get bored easily and don't show interest in most things.

- They put in effort into building a perfect image of themselves online, and they care a lot about the number of followers they have on their social media.

- Interactions online feel safer to them than interactions in real life.

An Example of a Vulnerable Narcissist

Since this type of narcissist is harder to identify, there might be a lot more vulnerable narcissists than we all realize. As an example, let's talk about Christina's case. She is a younger sister to one other girl, Kate. The relationship between the two sisters always had its ups and downs, just like any siblings' relationship, but these swings were often caused by Christina's own emotional swings.

Sometimes, she could keep a good relationship with Kate, but whenever her sister achieved something and made her parents proud, she would take offense at the fact that they did not praise her as much. She would make it about her by accusing their parents of not giving both girls the same opportunities when in reality Kate simply had more willpower.

One day, Kate decided to confront Christina about her behavior toward her and their parents, to which Christina responded with passive-aggressiveness and ended the conversation by saying that she could not take it anymore and that she was going to self-harm, storming off to the bedroom. Kate ended up feeling really guilty because she didn't want to see her sister suffering even though it was all because of Christina's mind games.

Christina shows clear signs of vulnerable narcissism. She is jealous of her sister's achievements. She blames her parents for something that is, in fact, her own fault, and she uses mind games and isolation to manipulate her sister's emotions.

As for the subtypes, there are five that originate from the three main types I just described, and they are the following:

Cerebral Narcissism vs. Somatic Narcissism

This is the first duality, and it is based on what the person uses to show others their superiority and get admiration back—that is, to get their narcissistic supply. Some narcissists go for their intellect (the cerebral narcissists) while others like to show off their physique (the somatic ones). *Soma* comes from the ancient Greek, and it means "body."

Common Traits of a Cerebral Narcissist

- They are very intelligent (or at least they pretend to be).
- They want everyone to admire them for their intellect.
- They often occupy authority positions.
- They are extremely confident, and that allows them to be very manipulative.
- They have no sexual interest toward other

people and prefer masturbation instead.

- They have life crises constantly.

- They love to brag about their academic and/or professional achievements.

- They often use complicated words in their day-to-day speech.

- They only want to befriend people who are as intellectually gifted as them, but because they don't actually believe anyone is as smart as them, they lie in order to build relationships and get their victims. Once they find a victim and build a rapport with them, they will often start to disengage and might become abusive toward them.

Common Traits of a Somatic Narcissist

- They always put in the effort to look their best.

- They are very interested in exercising, fitness, and dieting.

- They are obsessed with how they look and need everyone to notice them for their figure.

- They act as if they were celebrities.

- They live to get compliments on their looks.

- They give their "friends" backhanded compliments about their appearance.

- They are very sexually active, but the other person's body is nothing more than a sex toy to them. During intercourse, it is all about receiving pleasure and not giving it to the other person as well.

- They love to brag about their sexual encounters.

- They often use sex to control others because it is such an intimate moment where the other person becomes very vulnerable.

- In female somatic narcissists, it is not uncommon to like the idea of being the other woman.

- They are often considered to be hypochondriacs.

- They are fans of cosmetic surgery.

- They have very pricey buying habits even if they don't have the means to actually afford it. This might get them into a situation of debt, but the most important thing for them is to have expensive material things to show off.

An Example of a Cerebral Narcissist vs. an Example of a Somatic Narcissist

Fred and Jake are cousins. They are like polar opposites, but there is one thing that they have in common, and that is their inflated sense of self. They have always bragged about different things. Jake would always consider himself to be the most intelligent person in his family because he had good grades and attended both the math club and the science club in school, which nobody in his family had done before. He would use that grandiosity to manipulate his parents into getting everything he wanted. Fred, on the other hand, was obsessed with how he looked. He would always dress to show off his giant muscles and brag about different girls he hooked up every week. Both cousins show traits of narcissism, but because they show it in different ways, their subtypes of narcissism are different: Jake is a cerebral narcissist, and Fred is a somatic narcissist.

Can a Person be Cerebral and Somatic Simultaneously?

In fact, most narcissists present characteristics from both subtypes, but one is always more prominent than the other. They usually show signs of each subtype according to the circumstances of the situation they are in.

Overt Narcissism vs. Covert Narcissism

The second duality is based on how easy it is for others to notice someone's narcissism. *Overt* means "done or shown openly" while *covert* means "not openly acknowledged or displayed." So you can have an idea of what each of the subtypes means.

Common Traits of an Overt Narcissist

- They are easy to pinpoint.

- They are exhibitionists and extroverts.

- They clearly want to be the center of attention at all times.

- They love showing off pretty much anything: material possessions, their appearance, intellectual achievements, their financial status—you name it.

- They can easily feel offended by criticism (real or made up in their own mind).

- They always demand a lot from people.

- They are over-ambitious.

- They often maintain insincere relationships with others. They don't believe anyone is as good as them, so no one deserves their true love (whichever type of love it is—this doesn't just apply to romantic relationships).

- They are very charismatic.

- They have very strong opinions and take any chance they can to share them.

Common Traits of a Covert Narcissist

- They are not as easy to spot.

- They are usually shy and introverted, and they lack self-confidence.

- They are not ostentatious, but instead, feel like the world should be able to see how special they are. Because that doesn't happen, they feel like they are victims.

- They get extremely jealous of other people's victories.

- They get bored easily.

- They are not good listeners and tend to zone out whenever they don't find someone interesting enough to have their attention (which happens frequently).

- They lie constantly.

- They learn and rehearse what they are supposed to say to come off as a nice, compassionate person.

- They are observers more than they are doers or sayers.

- They are very judgmental and disinterested, which is easy to realize by the body movements, sounds, and facial expressions they make during interactions with others.

- In circumstances of conflict, they tend to be passive-aggressive. They never show how much a negative situation really affects them; instead, they act with dishonest indifference.

- They have a hard time establishing and nourishing authentic connections with others.

An Example of an Overt Narcissist vs. an Example of a Covert Narcissist

Solange and Carter both work at an online marketing agency. Solange is a very quiet developer who cannot seem to fit in with the rest of the developers even after two years of working in the agency. Most times, she has lunch by herself, but on the rare occasions when she joins her coworkers to eat, they all have a very hard time including her in the conversations as she never seems to be really present and often responds with one-word replies to any question directed to her. Everyone sees her as an introvert, and they often give up on trying to befriend her, which makes her feel like a victim in the workplace.

Carter, however, is the exact opposite. He's the new designer in the agency, and everyone loves how charismatic he is. In his last workplace, everyone also loved him in the beginning, but with time, they started to see another side to him. Once he became more comfortable in the team, he started demanding too much from everyone and getting angry when they didn't meet his standards. He stopped playing in the team (as he was dishonestly doing in the beginning to get people to trust him) and started focusing solely on himself, trying to get the boss's attention only on his "amazing" work. This will also happen in this new agency, and soon, people will clearly see him as a narcissist.

Because of how obvious Carter's self-centeredness is, he is considered to be an overt narcissist. Solange, on the other hand, is clearly a covert narcissist. People don't really notice her self-absorbance; they only see it as shyness.

Inverted Narcissism

The last subtype refers to the narcissists who are dependent on other narcissists (the so-called primary narcissists) and who feel an overblown need for their love and attention. Inverted narcissists, also known as narcissist-codependent, are unable to live their lives independently or draw their own individual path without the constant aid of another narcissist. An inverted narcissist is generally of the covert type, and they can either be somatic or cerebral, according to what they look for in the primary narcissist.

Common Traits of an Inverted Narcissist

- They feel the need for a relationship with a narcissist so bad that they can close their eyes to any abuse they might be undergoing.

- They need other people's input and opinions in order to make decisions.

- They are unable to take responsibility for their actions, especially the most critical ones.

- They are not comfortable with confrontation, so they don't start it. They also don't engage when others do.

- They need approval from others.

- They have no initiative because they don't believe in themselves. Even if deep down, they want to do or start something, they won't because of their extremely low self-esteem.

- They have a hard time saying no.

- They don't like being alone. In the romantic scope, this causes them to jump from relationship to relationship even if the feelings are not genuine because of their fear of being single.

- Emotionally, they are highly fragile.

- They feel like they don't deserve good things, but they daydream a lot about a life of power and success. They are immensely jealous of those who have achieved the life they fantasize about.

- They hate being the center of attention.

Narcissistic Personality Disorder (NPD)

So, we have learned that there are several types and subtypes of narcissists. However, that is not the only thing that distinguishes them from one another. The severity in which people feel and show their narcissistic traits makes the difference between it being a type of personality and a mental condition named narcissistic personality disorder. Let's dive into how this condition is different from narcissism and what its causes, symptoms, and consequences are.

What Is the Difference between Narcissism and Narcissistic Personality Disorder?

We are all narcissistic in some way, yet not all of us suffer from a narcissistic personality disorder. In fact, in 2005 only 0.5% of the American general population had the condition (Ambardar, 2018).

The main difference between a narcissist and someone who suffers from a narcissistic personality disorder is that the first one does not suffer from a mental illness and can function and achieve their goals while simply being seen by others as annoying, stuck up, and sometimes even evil. For the second one, it is not that simple. What goes on in the mind of someone who suffers from a narcissistic personality disorder is a lot more complicated, and so are the consequences that the condition has in their life. However, just like for any mental illness, these people can search for psychological help that will support them to overcome the disorder.

What Are the Causes of Narcissistic Personality Disorder?

It is hard to pinpoint exactly what leads to the development of the disorder, but there are three main groups of factors that can greatly influence the chances of someone developing narcissistic personality disorder—their upbringing as a child, their genetic characteristics, and social-cultural factors.

Childhood

A child is naturally selfish in the sense that they have certain wants and needs and will often throw a tantrum when those are not satisfied without putting into consideration the wants and needs of other people. With the education of parents and teachers, the child learns the concepts of altruism, empathy, and self-worth. The rule of thumb is that, as they grow, they become less selfish and more aware of how others are feeling. They acknowledge the importance of a balance between their self-worth and the worth of others and hopefully work toward maintaining it.

But alas, the rule of thumb doesn't apply to every single case, and some situations that people go through as infants may lead them to adopt narcissistic behaviors in the future and develop a narcissistic personality disorder.

- *If the parents worship the child and they never get any kind of repercussion due to negative behavior.* An example would be if a kid was bullying a classmate at school but the parents blamed the teacher for putting the two kids in the same classroom instead of disciplining their child.

- *If the parents never show appreciation for anything that the kid does and run the house in an environment of constant competition.* Parents who respond to their child's achievements with a "Why didn't you do better than that?" (for example, saying "Why didn't you get 100%?" as a reaction to a 99% score) are the perfect example of this.

- *If the parents have narcissistic behaviors regarding their child.* This would be the type of parent who takes any chance they can to brag about their child, often in an exaggerated way. This gives the kid a false sense of self-confidence, making them believe from a very young age that they are above everyone else, or it can make the kid grow up to develop an unhealthy view on their flaws and use narcissism as a mask to that insecurity.

- *If the parents are abusive toward them.* Abuse has severe psychological effects on anyone; in this case, those effects can culminate in the development of narcissistic traits.

Genetics

There are also studies that have proven the correlation

between a person's genetics and their predisposition to the progression of a narcissistic personality disorder. Research carried out by the *Journal of Psychiatric Research* in 2013 was the first one to prove that there are abnormalities commonly seen in the brain of a person with NPD. By studying the gray matter of a group of people, both with and without the condition, they came to the conclusion that people with narcissistic personality disorder have a smaller gray matter in the left anterior insula, which is directly linked to their emotional empathy levels (*Journal of Psychiatric Research*, 2013).

Culture

Typically, cultures that are most individualistic and competitive end up having a higher number of people who suffer from a narcissistic personality disorder. On the other hand, cultures that value community over individual tend to have fewer people with the condition. Let's take the United States and Saudi Arabia as two examples. The first one is commonly referred to as the "culture of narcissism" while the second is one of the most empathetic in the world. The two are like complete opposites in terms of the importance of self, comparing to that of others.

What Are the Symptoms of Narcissistic Personality Disorder?

It's important to know which signs you should look for in order to assess if someone simply has a narcissistic personality or if they do in fact suffer from a narcissistic personality disorder. What you need to look out for are the traits of a narcissist but in a more intense and persistent way. In a patterned way, that dictates each action, reaction, and decision they make; and that ends up damaging the person's ability to function like a "normal" person. Below are some common symptoms:

- They show the typical narcissist grandiose sense of self.

- They set unrealistic goals, both for themselves and others.

- They believe that those around them envy their life.

- They believe they deserve constant appraisal and recognition from others even when there is no reason for it.

- When they talk about their relationships, it is all about the "I" and not the "us."

- They cannot take criticism in a healthy way because they take everything personally. Even the slightest disagreement is often met with an overreaction.

- They always put the blame on others.

- They don't ever show remorse or empathy. This one is a big one to set the self-centered people apart from the people with the condition because the lack of empathy of someone with NPD is often a scary thing to witness.

- They are not able to take responsibility for their mistakes and flaws.

- They are very resistant to behavioral changes.

- They daydream and fantasize a lot.

- They are bullies.

- They only want to associate with people who they believe are as good as them. More often than not, no one meets this standard.

However, there are also the internal symptoms, which include loneliness, exaggerated self-criticism, a sense of inferiority, shame, and extreme sensitivity—in other words, the opposite of what they show to the world.

Obviously, most of the time, these symptoms are unknown to others, but by being aware of them, you can put the pieces together and pay attention to details on the person's behavior and speech that you normally wouldn't notice. This way, it might be easier for you to understand what the other person is going through.

When someone has these characteristics that lead them to adopt evil, harmful behaviors, hurting others with no empathy or compassion and taking on dangerous behaviors, that someone possibly has narcissistic personality disorder. So when you encounter someone whose narcissism feels like it's been multiplied by a lot, you should definitely look out for yourself and avoid becoming the person's victim. If the person who seems to suffer from the condition is a loved one, consider trying to get them professional help. NPD is difficult to treat but not impossible.

It is important to note, however, that the diagnosis of any mental condition is not something to be taken lightly. So you can never be 100% sure if someone has NPD or not until a specialized psychologist has evaluated the person and reached a conclusion. This means that the prior list of symptoms is more of a "beware of" kind of list than a diagnosis one.

What Are the Consequences of Narcissistic Personality Disorder?

You know by now that having NPD has several consequences on someone's life. These consequences get worse as years go by, and if the condition remains untreated, they debilitate the person from having a regular life. But what are these consequences exactly?

Mental Consequences

Depression

People with NPD expect to be successful in every possible way, and they have very high expectations for their lives. However, those of us who don't suffer from the condition know that nobody's life is perfect. We all go through setbacks. So people who have an unrealistic idea of what their life is supposed to be don't know how to react to obstacles in a healthy manner. The huge contrast between their dream life and reality makes them have very low lows, often leading to depression. This is especially common on narcissists of the vulnerable type.

Anxiety

Narcissists need attention and approval. This makes them feel a huge fear of being rejected and criticized, which makes them very nervous. When they are not assured by others of their grandiosity, their anxiety rises, so this is a very common mental condition for people with NPD. Besides that, the fact that they cannot always get their narcissistic supply (i.e., the approval and attention of others) is a big source of anxiety and paranoia, and if they go a long time without it, they might become depressed and even suicidal.

Another common disorder in people with NPD is social anxiety, particularly in covert narcissists, as they don't like interacting with others.

Social Consequences

Difficulty maintaining (and even starting) honest, meaningful relationships

When narcissists engage in a relationship with someone, what they want is to take advantage of them instead of connecting with them in a meaningful way. Their concern is "How can I can use this individual to get to my goal?" instead of "How can we, together, build a relationship that is beneficial for both of us?" This is the perfect recipe for disaster, and what is most likely to end up happening is either the "victim" who's being used finds a way of escaping the relationship because it doesn't fulfill them emotionally or the narcissist gets bored, doesn't see the victim as useful to them anymore, and moves on to the next person. This applies not only to romantic relationships but also to friendships and work relationships.

Loneliness

When we combine their difficulty in nourishing meaningful relationships with their impossible-to-meet standards for their peers, it is easy to understand why most people with NPD lead a very lonely life. It is like they are in a vicious cycle. They constantly feel lonely and rejected, yet they don't have the tools to build authentic connections with others.

Abusive behaviors toward loved ones

Because they see their "loved ones" as objects, the relationships of a person with NPD are very much based on their manipulation. They believe that they need to control the other person in order for the relationship to go as they envision it, and they don't feel empathy for the other person's feelings about their connection, sometimes even enjoying making the other person feel bad. Besides, a lot of people with NPD react to the slightest bump on the road with anger since everything is seen as a personal attack. All this causes the manipulation and control to be done sometimes through physical and psychological abuse.

Can Narcissistic Personality Disorder Be Clinically Diagnosed?

The simple answer is yes. The more complex one is yes, but there are no specific scientific tests you can do in a lab to reach a conclusion; it is instead a matter of observing patterns in one's behavior, comparing it to the standard behavior of someone with the disorder.

That standard behavior has been established by the American Psychiatric Association in the Diagnosis and Statistical Manual of Mental Disorders (DSM-5), which states that the person being analyzed should meet the following criteria:

- They have considerable impairments in their personality functioning in terms of self-function (caused by identity issues or self-direction issues) and interpersonal functioning (caused by a lack of empathy or difficulties regarding intimacy).

- They have personality traits of antagonism (grandiosity and attention seeking).

- The personality functioning impairments are long-lasting and consistent in various circumstances.

- The personality functioning impairments and the personality traits are not the norms in their stage of development or socio-cultural surroundings.

- The impairments and traits are not caused by substance abuse or another medical condition.

Can You Grow out of Narcissistic Personality Disorder?

Growing out of NPD by yourself is a very, very hard thing to accomplish, especially because a lot of people who have it don't realize they do, and that it is damaging their quality of life. The condition becomes the norm. So "growing out of it" might not be the best expression to use here.

NPD can, however, be treated with the help of a professional. Psychotherapy is generally used to help individuals with this disorder (as it is for a lot of other personality disorders), more specifically psychodynamic psychotherapy. This kind of therapy allows the patient to really go back and remember their past experiences and try to pinpoint what in their past led to their current behaviors. So through psychodynamic psychotherapy, the person becomes more conscious of their behaviors, which is a powerful first step toward recovery.

Cognitive behavioral therapy (CBT) is also commonly used to treat NPD. The goal of CBT is to change harmful thought patterns that lead to harmful behaviors. Through CBT exercises and techniques, the patient learns how to cope with a negative feeling or situation and turn it into a positive one.

The therapist might also suggest the patient to start taking medication, like antidepressants or mood stabilizers, in case they show symptoms of depression, anxiety, suicidal thoughts or extreme impulsive behavior. However, there is no medication that specifically tackles NPD, so the goal would always be to minimize some of the person's symptoms.

The person can also complement the therapy and/or medication with the regular attendance of a support group, either in person or online. Talking to others who are in the same situation as yourself is always a nice extra help because you don't feel as alone as you used to in your struggle. This applies to people with NPD as well, so it can bring great benefits to their recovery.

There are even family support groups for the relatives

of a person with NPD. If you are one, consider attending. A person's recovery of any mental condition can be a lot smoother if they have a strong support system at home and live with people who know how to act in order to help them get better. Besides that, you can always talk about how having a person with NPD has affected your family's dynamics and you will get the support from people who are or have been in your shoes. So ultimately, support programs can be greatly advantageous for all parties involved.

Step 1: A Summary

1. **Internalize the concept of narcissism.** Exaggerated self-esteem, disregard for other people's feelings, difficulty taking criticism, and overall sense of superiority are the key signs that someone is a narcissist.

2. Pay attention to those around you and **see if you recognize any of the narcissism types and subtypes**. Look at their behavior, the way they show their superiority, and how obvious they are about it. Remember some people are covert narcissists, so you might not notice them

at first.

3. If you come to the conclusion that you know someone with narcissistic traits, try to understand if they simply have those traits but can function normally in society or if their behavior is severely affected by the narcissism and the traits are more intense and long-lasting than normal. In other words, **try to understand if a person suffers from a narcissistic personality disorder.**

4. If they do have NPD, **make sure you are safe**. These people can be abusive and dangerous, and even if they are someone you love and care for, if you let them pull you into their narcissistic mind games and make you their next victim, you will not be able to help them overcome their disorder.

5. If it is a loved one, **try to find a professional psychologist in your area** who can help them. Be aware of the fact that you will probably be met with a lot of resistance when you bring up the topic of therapy to the narcissist.

Step 2: Assess if You Have Narcissistic Personality Disorder

You have read an entire chapter explaining the concepts of narcissism and narcissistic personality disorder; and maybe you saw yourself in some of the traits, symptoms, and examples that have been described. NPD is not something that just happens to others. You might be the extreme narcissist in the life of your loved ones. The second step of this book is all about helping you acknowledge your own narcissistic features, understand how severe they are, and know whether you should seek help.

However, we should begin by reminding you that we are all narcissistic to a certain degree. Remember that narcissism is a spectrum. So the fact that sometimes you put yourself and your own needs and desires first does not make you an unhealthy narcissist. Knowing the difference between self-esteem and self-absorbance is essential when we speak about narcissism.

Note: although there is a difference between narcissism and narcissistic personality disorder, from now on in the book, when I use the word "narcissistic" and unless stated otherwise, I am mentioning people with extreme narcissism that negatively and severely affects their life—i.e., people with NPD.

Questions to Ask Yourself

You will only know for sure if you have NPD when a certified professional assesses that you do; nevertheless, there are self-analysis exercises you can do to understand how high the chances that you do have it are. You have to be honest with yourself when you answer the questions; otherwise, the final results will not reflect the reality. Some things might be hard to admit, but doing so is the first step toward recovery.

- Do you feel a constant need to impress strangers?

- Do you see yourself as more than those around you in every situation?

- Do you set unrealistic expectations to your loved

ones, as well as new people you meet, and end up withdrawing when they don't meet them?

- Do you take any chance you can to brag about your achievements?

- Do you have a hard time getting negative feedback even if it is constructive?

- Do you find yourself reacting angrily when people disagree with you?

- Do you believe people should always be there for you no matter what is going on in their lives?

- Do you constantly fantasize about a life filled with power and success?

- Do you have a hard time feeling compassion about a situation when it does not have a direct negative effect on yourself?

- Do you feel like everyone is out to get you?

- Do you, deep inside, have very low self-esteem?

If you responded affirmatively to most of the questions and you feel like these traits have a big impact on the quality of your life and relationships with others, you might want to consider beginning your recovery process. We will cover how you can do it soon.

A Test Approved by Professionals

If you google "NPD test," you will find a lot of different quizzes that promise to let you know if you have the disorder or not. There is not a specific one that is globally accepted by psychotherapists, but if you go through the results, you will find some that will at least get you to become more aware of the way you function. One example would be the [Narcissistic Personality Inventory](), which I invite you to take. However, you should never take the result of an online quiz as a definite diagnosis, so if you want to be sure, definitely schedule an appointment with a professional.

Which Steps Should I Take if I Have NPD?

The recovery process for NPD is similar to that of other personality disorders, such as borderline personality disorder or antisocial personality disorder. Getting better is hard work and takes time and patience, so you should internalize that this process will require a lot from you and it will not happen overnight. This is easier to do if you focus on the improvements you will feel in the long run—better management of emotions, better relationships, and better overall functioning in life.

There are four major steps to this recovery:

1. Acknowledgment of the narcissistic traits and consequent damage

It is popular knowledge that the first step to getting better is admitting that we have a problem, and NPD is no exception to that. The good news is that, if you responded to the questions above or took an online test and got a result that indicated that you might suffer from NPD, you already started working on this first stage of recovery. You might feel tempted to give up because getting better means being honest and vulnerable and admitting to things you have been working so hard to hide.

But it is crucial, in order to continue the process, to be able to look at this issue as something you have the power to beat instead of something that brings you shame. Mental disorders are very common, and you probably know people who have one (maybe even someone who has NPD). With the proper motivation and work, it is possible to overcome these conditions and achieve a better quality of life.

2. An honest pursuit of support from your loved ones

This step can be very hard. No one likes to admit that they are struggling internally and that that struggle is damaging their lives. As someone with NPD, you are probably not used to taking responsibility and assuming something that might be seen as a weakness. Take the opportunity to look at this step as your first exercise against your narcissism. Instead of perceiving the act of opening up as something you don't want to do because you don't want to admit to your flaws, look at it as an opportunity to show vulnerability. Let people know that, even though your behavior up to that point might not indicate so, you do have feelings deep inside you that you need help dealing with.

This step may require some patience and understanding from your part—again, things you are not used to feeling toward other people. Your NPD has possibly caused you to bully, humiliate, or even abuse the people in your life. Behaviors as such leave marks in those relationships, and not everyone will react to your request for help with open arms. People might need time, and you should take that to not only tell them but also show them that you are ready to get better.

If you find yourself completely alone, you can look for online forums with people who struggle or have struggled with NPD. Although it is not the same as having someone literally by your side who gives you strength and courage for you to keep working toward your final goal, associating with people who understand what you feel and who have successfully overcome their problems should serve as an inspiration to keep going even when it seems pointless.

3. Searching for a professional in your area

This third step can be done at the same time as the second one, particularly if you don't receive the immediate support from the people you opened up to. Actively starting to look for professional help by yourself shows that you have the willpower to give recovery a try. In fact, you can even do it before talking to your loved one, if you feel strong enough to take that step by yourself.

What you should look for is either a psychotherapist or a CBT therapist as those are the two big types of therapy used to treat NPD. Try to find one in your area that is within your budget, but if you can't find one that meets your criteria, you can also look for online therapy. Be sure to look for reviews from the therapist's previous clients and to go for a professional who has a relevant certification in therapy. Going for someone who has previously dealt with NPD can also be a good idea, but you might not be able to find one that easily.

4. Adoption of coping techniques in day-to-day life

With your therapist, you will learn ways of being in control of your emotions, changing your negative reactions and behaviors, and starting and nourishing meaningful connections, as well as fixing damaged ones. But as much as you learn and as much effort as you put into your sessions, if you don't apply those learnings to your life, there is no point.

The first step to being able to do so is accepting your diagnosis. Once you do it, it becomes a lot easier for you to pinpoint situations where you might be allowing your NPD to take over your thinking process. Being able to recognize those situations and having the necessary tools to turn them around gives you the ability to control your narcissistic tendencies instead of letting them control you.

How Can I Change the Narcissistic Patterns in My Life?

Besides going to the therapist (and possibly a support group), there are things in your daily life that you can work on toward becoming a more compassionate and less egoistic person. This is all easier said than done (if it were easy to do, you would not be where you are), but with the proper support system and will to improve, the tips I am about to tell you are all attainable. And of course, as you go forward in your therapy, everything will just keep getting easier until it becomes organic.

- **Listen more.** Be aware of when you start to speak too much and ask a question to the other person regarding what you were speaking about. Don't judge the other person on their reply. Having an open mind will be very valuable not only to your relationships with others but also to your relationship with yourself.

- **Make a conscious effort to care about people** and their feelings and to act accordingly.

- **If you tell someone you will do**

something, go through with it. If you know you can't commit to doing it, don't lie. If you think you can do it but you need help, ask for help. If you make a promise and don't keep it, assume the responsibility. Honesty is the best policy, and people are a lot more understanding and forgiving than you might think.

- **Accept that because you are human, you will fail.** Accept the imperfection of life and the setbacks you will encounter. Look at mistakes as opportunities to learn instead of shameful failures.

- **Find exercises and techniques that you can do when you start to get anxious** and/or angry to counteract those feelings.

- **Become mindful of your behavior** and of when your narcissistic traits start to come up and apply the coping mechanisms that you and your therapists found to be most effective in your case.

- **Find something that you can do that provides you with the same satisfaction as when you belittle and humiliate others.** Direct your energy toward something positive without compromising the enjoyment you get from it.

- **Take time to get to know yourself emotionally** and understand what positive things, like friendship, love, success, and happiness, mean to you once you take the narcissistic mask off.

- **Set realistic life objectives** and find a method to work toward them in a healthy, efficient, and honest manner.

Step 2: A Summary

5. Assess your behavior and try to **pinpoint any constant, long-lasting traits** or behaviors that might indicate that you have NPD.

6. Search for an **online quiz that looks reliable and based on trustworthy sources** and take it. Remember, this is not an official diagnosis but something that might give you an idea of what you should do next.

7. If you come to the conclusion that you need

help, try to **get in the best mindset** for recovery that you can.

8. **Open up to your loved ones.** Having external support will help you a lot. Be patient with them as they might be hurt by some of your previous actions.

9. Look for a professional therapist and **work toward recovery every day.**

Step 3: Assess Who Is the Narcissist in Your Life

It is also possible that, as you read the first chapter of the book, you didn't see yourself in it but you saw someone who is close to you. In situations where you might be the victim or you just know someone who is a narcissist, it is just as important to know how to proceed—firstly, because you need to protect yourself from this person, and secondly, because they might need help and you can be the one to give them the support they are lacking.

Narcissism in other people might exist in all sorts of relationships. In this chapter, we will cover four of them—romantic relationships, friendships, family, and work relationships. We will tell you the signs to look for in each of those, but keep in mind that they are only a sign of extreme narcissism if they do it constantly and for a long time. If they did it once or twice, they are most likely not a narcissist but had one or two narcissistic moments.

Narcissists are not automatically monsters. As you have realized throughout the book, they are typically in a lot of internal pain. So unless you are in a situation that is harmful or even a threat to your safety, try not to demonize the narcissist you are dealing with. If they are honestly willing to get better, try to be there for them without becoming a victim to their abuse or manipulation.

But if they don't have that determination to change, know that it is not on you to convince them to get help. If this person has mean, aggressive, or even abusive behaviors toward you, your only concern should be to get out of the situation safely.

Narcissism in Your Relationship

The first type of relationship I will talk about is the romantic one. If you are dating a narcissist, there is a cycle of three stages that you probably experienced (or are experiencing right now). Of course, each relationship is one of a kind (and so is each narcissist), so this doesn't mean that every single one goes through these exact stages. Some skip one; others have one or more extra stages. However, these three are the standard ones, so we will focus on them.

Stage 1: The Idealization (or "I Love You So Much!") Phase

The first stage is the one where your partner gets your attention by showing you unconditional love and affection—sometimes even a little too much. It is commonly called the "love bombing" phase, which is definitely an expression that does justice to it. The narcissist will tell you that you are the one for them, that this is it, true love in its purest form; yet they don't really believe that. By now, the narcissist has figured out how to be the person you have always dreamed of, and that is who they become. This means that they will be on the same wave as you, have the same dreams and aspirations, and just overall seem like the perfect person to build a future with.

At this point, the narcissist idolizes you. You are the only thing they see, think, and talk about. They seem almost obsessed, but you see it as just intense love. They put you on a pedestal, compliment you constantly, and make you fall for all the attention and devotion that you are getting. Together, you make all these plans for the future, and you go on the most romantic dates and vacations. Plus, the sex is amazing.

You don't suspect that their words and actions are dishonest, and you slowly fall deeply in love with this person (or better yet, with the person that they are pretending to be). After all, this is how all great love stories begin—with the honeymoon phase, the phase when both of you only have eyes for each other and when life is perfect.

In the idealization phase, your relationship feels like a fairy tale, and when you are living it, it is almost impossible to figure out that the person you are falling in love with is actually an extreme narcissist. This is because there are no real signs for suspicion, and even if there are, you are on cloud nine, so chances are, you won't see them. You might think that what you are experiencing is too good to be real but not to the point of actually distrusting your partner's intentions.

This phase is essential to the narcissist as their victim, over time, lets their guards down, becoming completely vulnerable to them, which is the necessary state for the following stages.

Stage 2: The Devalue (or "You Are Not That Great") Phase

So the narcissist finally feels like they have total control over you, that your happiness and well-being are in their hands. This is when the second stage begins—the stage where you suddenly are not enough for them anymore. Usually, this phase starts to be noticeable very gradually, but you can definitely see the shift happening. This is very confusing to the victim because, during the first stage, they put all their trust in their partner, and when the relationship seems to be very healthy and stable, this shift happens.

They throw you off the pedestal, the compliments are replaced with harsh criticism, and the fairy tale turns into a nightmare. You don't go on dates anymore, and the sex might start slowing down or being all about the narcissist and their needs. The narcissist becomes cruel, angry, and over controlling of you; but because you are so deeply in love with them, you downplay their behavior. Even if your friends and relatives try to talk to you about it (which by phase 2 is bound to happen), you close your eyes to the reality of the situation you are in.

And it is not just toward you that the narcissist's anger is directed. In social situations, the narcissist will not make any efforts into getting along with people, and they will make it clear as water that they do not like those who are present and they do not want to be there.

Because of this behavior, you will probably not go to as many social happenings, even with close friends and family. On the one hand, your partner might manipulate you into saying no to such invitations, and on the other hand, as much as your friends and relatives love you, it is hard to endure the bullying of your partner, and that might affect your own relationships that existed before you met the narcissist in your life.

Even if nobody directly asks you to, the second phase of your relationship is where you will have to choose between your partner and your friends and family. Unfortunately, because the narcissist now has such control over you, you will most likely choose them. It is almost like you are a puppet and the narcissist is the puppeteer, so the fact that you chose them over your loved ones is not entirely your own decision but the decision that the circumstances led you to make.

By this phase, even though you are not happy with your relationship, your partner is probably the person you spend the most time with because they make you isolate yourself more and more. For them, this means that they have more time to criticize, belittle, and abuse you and, therefore, showcasing and proving to themselves their (imagined) superiority.

Stage 3: The Discard (or "You Are Not Good Enough for Me Anymore") Phase

After they strip you of your self-esteem, it is time for the narcissist to abandon you. The third stage comes when they realize that you are not useful to them as a supply anymore, and thus, it is time for them to find their next victim, whom they will idolize just as much as they once idolized you. You stop being useful when you stop giving them the attention and devotion that they need to feed the false image of superiority that they have been building or when you threaten said image. The slightest thing you say or do might be a trigger for this person to discard you, like you disagreeing with something they said or trying to stick up for yourself when they are abusing you.

For a narcissist, maintaining a relationship only makes sense while they feel like they are the leader and everything happens on their terms. They know that, just like you did, someone else will fall for their idealization phase, so it is not hard for them to leave you. Plus, if you show them that you are hurting, that feeds their narcissism, and that is a reason for them to stay away.

This phase is really painful, as any breakup is, especially considering how in love the narcissist made you fall for them and how much they hurt your self-love. However, it is your chance to finally escape, and it is as such that you must see it. Hopefully, you will have people who will still accept you back even after the narcissist made you cut ties with them. Find support in them, and as much as you are hurting, don't show it to the narcissist. Work to become your true self again and to get over how much this relationship has damaged you.

After a while, the narcissist might try to get you back, so it is crucial that you use your single time to get out of the victim role you have been playing in your relationship and get back in control of your own life, decisions, and actions. When you do this, even if not fully, it becomes easier for you to resist your ex-partner's attempts of getting back together with you.

What Are the Warnings Signs to Look Out For?

Although the three stages I described above are the norm when someone is in a relationship with a narcissist, they might not always be easy to recognize, especially if you are living them first-hand. You might be in such awe of this person that you close your eyes to their behavior without even noticing you are doing it, or you might even acknowledge it but continuously try to excuse your partner's actions.

It is crazy how chameleon-like narcissists can be, but it is not impossible to spot patterns in their behavior. As was mentioned, on the first stage it is hard to notice that anything is wrong in the relationship, but there are some red flags that can happen as early as on the first date:

- **The conversation (that is not really a conversation but a monologue) between you two is mostly about him or her.** There is no real interest in hearing your stories and opinions; and anything that is being discussed always goes back to them, their life, and their experiences. However, they never really go into much detail when they talk about themselves, and in the end, you will know a lot but all on the surface level.

- **They complain a lot.** Even the smallest thing that goes wrong will cause an overreaction. Because they expect to receive special treatment everywhere they go, they get disappointed constantly, which means a whole lot of complaining.

- **They are very impatient.** If you go to a restaurant and your food takes a little longer to get to the table than usual, it is enough to set off their bad mood, and again, they will complain and overreact.

- **They will want 150% of your attention.** If you notice something or someone else, they will do anything to bring your attention back to them and what they were saying.

- **They lead the date.** Even if you make a suggestion, they find a way of saying that you should do what they want instead. They want to be in control from the get-go.

- **They take any chance they can to check how they look.** Anything that makes the slightest reflection is a mirror to the narcissist.

- **The chemistry between the two of you is crazy** because they know how to build an exciting, heated atmosphere of romance from day one.

But a first date is rarely ever enough for someone to make such a big assumption as "The person I went out with is a narcissist." Even with all the warning signs, it is easy for the new victim to brush them off because the narcissist is so charismatic and charming.

However, on the second stage, those warning signs start to become a lot more evident to those around you, and they can become evident to you as well if you know what to look for in your partner's demeanor.

- Your feelings are never taken into account in the relationship.

- Everything negative that happens in the relationship is your fault, and there's no arguing with them.

- To them, it is more important how people perceive you as a couple than how your relationship actually is.

- They are not close to anyone, and they don't make an effort to get along with the people you are close with.

- They don't care about your safety.

- They never congratulate you for your victories or feel happy for you. Instead, they might make you feel like you could have done better.

- They always have an opinion on your outfits, makeup, hair, or body shape (and it is never positive).

- Independently of how much effort you put into the relationship and into making them happy, they always feel like you could do more, and they don't try to hide that away from you.

- They try to force their own opinions, ideas, and beliefs on you no matter how many times you tell them that you do not agree (or try to tell them, as they will not give you a lot of airtime to express how you feel about what they are saying).

- Because of how critical and brutally honest they are, after a while, it starts to affect your self-esteem. They make you feel bad about yourself because of their own unrealistic expectations.

The Concept of Codependency

Codependency is the reason why a lot of relationships with narcissists work (and by work, I mean work for the narcissist only). Codependent people are individuals who always put others in front of them, who live to please and make other people's wishes and desires come true. They need to feel needed and useful to others. Just like with narcissism, codependency is a sign of an unbalanced sense of self. These people do not see their own value, and they live their lives accordingly.

They don't know how to set boundaries as to what others can ask from them since they have set for their ultimate life goal to serve others even if it means putting themselves in unfavorable and even dangerous situations.

Narcissism and codependency are described as complete opposites. Narcissists need someone who devotes their time to please and praise them and make them feel like the superior image of themselves that they have built in their own minds is actually real. So narcissism and codependency are like two pieces of a puzzle that fit perfectly together even though it is a puzzle of an unhealthy, unbalanced, harmful relationship, particularly for the codependent person. Codependent people are the perfect victims for narcissists, and the manipulation skills of a narcissist are the utmost trap for a codependent person.

Codependency is a real problem that requires real attention. If you suspect from your previous (or current) relationships that you might suffer from it, you can reach out for help from an online support group, a therapist, or even a group (e.g., Co-Dependents Anonymous). Talk to someone you trust about your problem and start your recovery process.

A Narcissist "Love" Story: An Example

Michael had never had much luck in his love life, and he was not very good at meeting new people even though he longed for love and for the opportunity to make someone as happy as possible. He decided to give dating apps a try, and one day he came across Stephanie's profile. He could tell right away that she took really good care of her looks, with amazing outfits and makeup, and that she was a fitness aficionado. The two ended up matching on the dating app, and after a couple of days of chatting, they decided it was time to meet up. For their first date, Michael suggested a small restaurant that was halfway from where each of them lived, but Stephanie did not like the idea and suggested they would go to one of the hip restaurants in town, so Michael agreed.

They went for dinner, and when it was over, Michael knew a lot about Stephanie but felt like he did not really have the chance to tell her about him. "She is probably just more extroverted than I am. Next time, I'm sure I'll get to participate more," he thought. And so they went on more dates, and every time, Stephanie made him feel like he was the most powerful, most successful, most attractive man on earth. Time went by, and they got into a serious relationship. Everything was perfect to the point that Michael decided it was time for him to propose to her. He was sure she was the one!

A few months into the marriage, Stephanie stopped idolizing Michael as much. Suddenly, he could use a gym subscription, they needed to go shopping for clothes that actually fit him, he could use a haircut, he should try harder at work, and he could use some improvements in bed. She manipulated him into stopping hanging out with family and friends because if he wanted their marriage to work, he needed to try harder to make her happy.

Nothing he did was good enough, and Michael didn't understand what happened because he did not change; he was acting as he did from the beginning. However, he started to believe that something was, in fact, wrong with him. Maybe he did start slacking off without even noticing. Isn't that what they say happens when you get married and settle down?

Meanwhile, Stephanie started being verbally abusive toward Michael, but he was so in love with her that he could not seem to be able to leave. He found someone who was everything he always wanted. How could he let go? Stephanie's dissatisfaction with Michael seemed to grow every day until one day she brutally broke up with him and asked for a divorce because he was not good enough for her anymore. She said she tried her hardest to make it work, so he was the only one to blame for the way everything ended.

Michael was left with his self-esteem shattered. He felt nothing but confusion as to when everything started to change. He felt guilty for abandoning his loved ones for a woman, but the love he still felt for her was indescribable. Michael was Stephanie's supply from day one, and once he stopped being useful, he was discarded. He was in a relationship with a narcissist and, in the end, was left to deal with the impact that had on him.

Narcissism in Your Family

Narcissism also exists in family relationships. We probably all have one relative who is a narcissist, but maybe not an extreme one and not a close relative. However, when this exaggerated self-absorbance exists on one of our direct family members, that can have a huge negative impact on the dynamic between relatives. Parents, siblings, and kids are the three family levels where narcissism affects a person the most because these are people who play (or should play) a giant role in their lives. But how exactly does NPD is these relatives affect a victim's well-being?

Narcissistic Parents

If one of your parents is a narcissist, they have probably caused you a lot of pain while you were growing up, and that has had its consequences on your own self-image as an adult. Narcissistic parents are unable to build a healthy relationship with their children, and to them, it is like their kids are invisible. That powerful tie that so many parents talk about that comes from this deep, unconditional love that they feel for their daughter or son—that does not exist for a narcissist parent. And that forces the child to grow up a lot faster than any kid should have to, because they don't receive the warmth and love that they should, at least over the first few years of their lives. These children grow up feeling unwanted, unloved, and less than; and those feelings never truly go away even if they choose to cut ties with their parents, which is hard to do for anyone, no matter how bad the parents are.

Signs You Were Raised by a Narcissistic Parent

As a child, the fact that you were being raised by a narcissist might not have been clear to you because you didn't know any other reality, so to you, the behavior that your parent showed was normal. As you grew up, you met other people and realized that maybe your childhood was not the most common or fair one. You recall certain situations and events and look at them with a different perspective because now you do know better.

You might feel like something about the way your parents brought you up was off, but not be able to pinpoint exactly what the issue was. The signs below are common traits and attitudes that a narcissistic parent has, so if you remember one of your parents constantly adopting them during your childhood, that might be it—your mother or father was a narcissist.

- From a very young age, **they made you act according to what those around you will think**. In everything they do, there is a worry regarding the image that they are constructing in the eyes of others, and they pass on that worry to you. They want the world to see you as the perfect family that everybody envies and wants to be a part of, and they need you to do your part from the start.

- **They are unable to feel your pain.** When something bad happens, the first instinct for most of us is to run to our parents' arms in search of support and love that only they can give us. If one of your parents was a narcissist, you have never had contact with such kind of support and love because they cannot give it. When something bad happened to you, they would respond with zero compassion and even some judgment.

- **You could not talk to them about anything emotional.** Because they are not in touch with their own emotions, they don't want you to feel like discussing feelings is healthy or needed. So they teach you to bottle things up and to hide all those emotions in the back of your mind.

- **They never respected your privacy.** They don't have any empathy of consideration for your feelings, and that can lead them to be too intrusive, either psychologically or physically. So if they want to know something about your life, they will do whatever it takes to find that out.

- **Your relationships within the direct family have never been balanced.** With your parents, this means that you have been taught from a young age that you exist to serve and praise them and make sure that their needs are being met instead of them doing anything and everything to make sure you are growing up to be a healthy and happy adult. It is almost like they needed that extra supply, and so they made you. But your relationship with your siblings might also be affected as the narcissistic parent will not want you to be close. They will instill an environment of rivalry between their kids instead of fostering a healthy relationship of true love and everlasting support for each other.

- **They lived their own dreams through you**—that is, they forced you into doing something that they have always wanted to do but never got around to. So they wanted you to be successful, not for yourself and doing what you love but for their own satisfaction and doing what they love.

- **They have used several manipulation techniques while you are growing up.** A couple of popular ones are the negative comparison (an example would be "Your classmate would never get a B. Why can't you be more like him?"), guilt trip (for instance, "I work all day every day to be able to give you everything you want, and you can't even do one thing for me?"), and shame (for example, "If you weren't so fat, people would love you more, but now I'm embarrassed to even go outside with you"). Narcissistic parents can be unbelievably cruel to their own children, and the way they act will always have an effect on the kids.

- **They expect you to take care of them forever.** The idea of you having your own life is not acceptable to them because your life should revolve around them until the second they pass away. Because it is so difficult to accept that your parent does not truly love you and because, even if it is not mutual, you probably feel a lot of love for your narcissistic mother or father, these expectations that they have may end up being fed until the end of their life.

One might wonder why a narcissist would ever want to become a parent if they are so focused on their own self. The answer to that questions is that, when a narcissist has a child, they are not thinking about the moments of happiness that they will spend with their kid or about how they will finally understand what unconditional love means. On the contrary, they are thinking about how they will not have to fight to have this human being's attention and devotion since being their mother or father automatically gives them power over the new child, at least until they are eighteen years old.

How Your Childhood Affected You

After reading the warning signs that someone is being brought up by a narcissistic parent, it is not hard to imagine how severe and long-lasting the consequences of their childhood can be. Children of narcissistic parents tend to grow into psychologically unbalanced people who have a damaged view of themselves. As adults, children of narcissists usually have the following characteristics:

- **They are unable to think for themselves** because they have never truly been allowed to be themselves but the person their parent wanted them to be. These kids were born for their parents to turn them into their "mini-me." So during their childhood, instead of having time to explore who they are and build their own personalities, they were turned into a younger version of their mother or father. These children don't have their own opinions, beliefs, passion, and overall personality because their parents did not allow them to figure out who they really are.

- **They feel a lot of self-hate and self-blame.** As kids, they didn't know better than to believe what their parents tell them. As these children were constantly being bombarded with their parents' negative opinions, after a while, they started to believe them. By the time they are adults, these ideas about themselves are so deeply internalized that it becomes very hard to change them.

- **They are scared of getting too in touch with their emotions and of opening up to others.** Just think about it: if you can't trust your own mother and father to be there for you and to treat you with the care and respect that you deserve, why would you put that kind of trust on anyone else? So growing up with narcissistic parents tends to result on insecure attachment (i.e., the inability to become close with someone in a healthy way), and that usually happens in one of two ways: anxious attachment, which is when someone who is constantly longing for more love but never feels like they are properly appreciated, which can lead them to become quite clingy and unconfident; or avoidant attachment, which is when someone does not want to be alone but also does not feel comfortable with another person getting too close to them, so they build emotional and physical walls in the relationship and don't ever let the partner in.

- **They become narcissists themselves**, especially when they are naturally stubborn. Their self-esteem is so broken that, when they realize that they will never beat their parents in their manipulative mind games, they end up giving in.

- **They suffer from mental health issues**, particularly when the parent was extremely abusive. The world becomes a very scary place when the people who are supposed to love you no matter what are the ones that hurt you the most, physically and/or psychologically. The scars that such experiences leave are unimaginable for most of us, but they often lead the person to live in constant fear, which can result in several mental illnesses, with post-traumatic stress disorder, anxiety, depression, and suicidal thoughts being four of the most common ones. In fact, a study conducted in February of 2019 revealed that people who had a close relative (or partner) who suffered from extreme narcissism showed high levels of mental illness: 69% were depressed and 82% had some kind of anxiety disorder (Day, Bourke, Townsend & Grenyer, 2019).

Being a Child of a Narcissist Parent: An Example

Martha and Alan had been in a relationship for a little over five years, and he decided it was time for them to have their firstborn. They start trying, and eventually, Martha gets pregnant. The baby is born, and they name her Sonia.

Sonia does not know it yet, but her childhood isn't going to be easy, and it is all due to Alan's narcissism. Alan was a receptionist at a gym (although he would always tell people he was one of the top managers there), but his real dream had always been to become a famous football player. Since it was too late for him, his wish was for their baby to be a boy so that he could turn him into the football player he got around to be.

The first moment he saw Sonia was the first moment he felt disappointed with his child. As she grew up, Alan would only allow her to wear boy clothes. He wanted a boy, and he was going to have one even if it meant that he had to force his daughter to be as boyish as possible. He put Sonia on the school football team, but she would always see her female colleagues playing tennis, and that was the sport she actually wanted to try.

Once, she tried saying that to her dad and was met with an angry, aggressive response. "I do everything I can to keep paying for your classes so you can continue in the school team, and your way of thanking me is by telling me you don't want to play football anymore?" Sonia feels guilty, so she continues to let her father shape her personality, beliefs, and opinions.

She tries going to Martha, her mother, for support. But Martha has always been a victim to Alan's lies and manipulation techniques, and that has harmed her ability to stand by her daughter and defend her. Marta's main objective is to keep Alan happy, and she knows that showing disagreement will do the exact opposite.

Years go by, and Sonia finally has the guts to move out

of her parents' home. Sonia deals with major anxiety and depression, and it is only when she meets her roommate, Tania, that she understands the impact that her childhood had on her. With the support of Tania, Sonia starts going to therapy and deals with the wounds she was left with, becoming a healthier and happier person.

Although Sonia's story had a happy ending, she had a very traumatic childhood, and some effects would never truly go away, all because of her father's insecurities masked with his narcissism.

Narcissistic Siblings

If the narcissist in your life was not one of your parents but your brother or sister, you probably grew up in an environment of constant bullying and extreme competitiveness from their end without your parents even having one single suspicion.

You probably lived in fear of being successful and never got to truly celebrate your victories. Living with a narcissistic sibling can be just as traumatic as living with a narcissistic parent, because we all have this idea of what a relationship between brothers and sisters should be like, yet in situations like this, the reality could not be more far off. You (and possibly other relatives) are nothing more than a "supply" to the narcissistic sibling. And you can't run away, at least not until you are old enough to move out of your parents home, so you know you will have no choice but to endure with your sibling's egoistic ways for a while. Once again, family dynamics are damaged, and so is the mental state of everyone involved.

Signs You Grew up with a Narcissistic Sibling

If you are the oldest sibling, you were probably excited when your parents announced that soon a new family member would arrive; and if you are a younger sibling, you certainly imagined what life would be like if your older brother or sister were there to protect you like they were supposed to.

When it is healthy, the connection between siblings is amazing, sometimes even unbreakable. But sadly, that is not always the case, and even though it is an unfortunate situation, it is crucial that you know the warning signs that can show you the narcissism of your sibling.

- **They act a certain way when they are with you, and then act a completely different way in front of other people.** As narcissists, lying and manipulating come naturally to them, so they can easily hide their true self from others. They become the most charming person on earth, deceiving everyone they meet.

- **If you confide something to them, they have no problems saying it to other family members.** Even if you don't tell them anything, they are constantly trying to find as much as they can about your life, whether it is by asking you or by asking your partner. All they want is material they can use against you.

- **They will make your relatives think of you as an unstable, crazy sibling, and they will act as if they were the victim** who has to deal with your mental imbalances. They will lie just to make you look bad in front of your family even if you are the most stable person on earth. And if you ever try to tell your relatives what is actually the reality (how manipulative, egoistic and cruel your sibling is), they will react with extreme anger.

- **They always want to compete with you.** Whenever you achieve something, their brain goes straight to "I can do better" instead of congratulating you and celebrating your victory by your side.

- **You don't feel comfortable around them.** In the beginning, you might not understand why, but every time you two hang out, you feel uneasy and like you just don't want to be there.

Having a narcissistic sibling can have a big negative impact on your reputation. They constantly bad-mouth and humiliate you in front of people. Since those around you know that the narcissist is your brother or sister, they don't see any reason as to why they would lie and paint a horrible image of you that, in fact, could not be further away from the truth. Your sibling knows how to control everyone in their life, and if you don't learn how to protect yourself from that, you can end up in very lamentable situations.

Narcissistic Kids

Children can also be narcissistic. This can be a result of genetic malformations, but more often than not, it comes from the way their parents bring them up. So if your kid is narcissistic, there is probably something about the way you or your partner treat them that you need to change in order to change their behavior. A child is still very easy to influence, so if you recognize from a young age that they are showing traits of narcissism, you are still in time to help them shift the way they act so that, eventually, they grow up to be healthy, balanced adults.

A child is not a fully developed human being, which means that you can't really say that they are a narcissist but rather a narcissist in the making. So if you notice that your child (or another kid in your life) is starting to showcase the traits of narcissism that we have been describing throughout this book in a constant, intense way, it is probably time to act on it. In the next chapter, I will cover some changes you can make as a parent in order to prevent your child from living the challenging life of a narcissist.

Narcissism in Your Friendships

We probably all have that one friend who is way too obsessed with him- or herself but whom we still love dearly because they have still been there for us when we needed them. They just speak a little too much about themselves. Sometimes it is actually fun and it causes a lot of laughter; other times we just use our secret technique of zoning out without them noticing that we have developed after so many years of having that person in our life. That is narcissism, but on an okay level of the spectrum, in a way that is not that detrimental for anyone.

However, that is not always the case. Some friendships become extremely toxic and abusive because of the narcissism of one of the parts.

Signs Your Friend Is Narcissistic

Just like in a romantic relationship, the narcissism in a friendship is not that noticeable from the start, especially when you are one of the victims. Things change over time, and their narcissistic ways start to become quite evident for everyone. It is hard to escape from a narcissistic friendship because you grew to be very fond of the other person. It is like a breakup on a different level. But staying in such a destructive friendship will never be good for you as hard as the departure may be at first.

So what do you need to look out for in order to discern if your friend is the narcissist in your life?

- **You can never give them advice.** In a normal friendship, two people are there for each other to hear the other one's struggles and try to give them some guidance regarding what to do next so that they will feel better. Not only is that guidance well received, but in a lot of cases, it is also asked for. Not with a narcissist. They see your attempt at giving them advice as a personal attack. They think you're telling them that there is something wrong with them. They cannot accept that you may think that they could deal with a certain situation in a better way or that they have space for improvement in a certain area of their life.

- **They also don't really give advice to you.** If you try to vent to them about something that is bothering you, they will quickly tell you that not only do they also have a problem, but theirs is way worse than yours. It is like a competition on whose life is harder, and the narcissist always wins.

- **You don't feel like hanging out with them like you used to.** When you first met this person, being around them was always fun. Even when you had a bad day, you knew if you went for a coffee with them, they would make you smile and laugh with their crazy stories. It was fun for you, so you gave them attention. What you didn't know was that the attention was exactly the supply they needed to feed their already giant ego. Once they realized that you saw them as a true friend, they knew they could start revealing their true self, so they start demanding more and more attention and even become controlling of you.

- **They bad-mouth people you both know.** This one is always a red flag, be it because of their narcissism or any other reason. It comes from the need to control you. They want you to give them your full attention, so they try to paint images of your other friends that are not real, with the intention of making you want to stop hanging out with them. Think about it: if they gossip about your friends and talk trash about them behind their backs, what makes you think that they would not do the same to you? People like this are definitely not to trust.

- **It is impossible for you to have a conversation with them where you both get to participate equally.** It is not a teaching and learning experience for both parts. Narcissists have no interest in getting to know your perspective on things, so they will dominate the conversation because they know for a fact that the way they see and think about things is the best possible way. Even in situations where you start the dialogue, in the end, they found a way of taking the lead and making it all about them.

A narcissist does not see friendship as a relationship where both people are equal and both win with the connection in terms of happiness, good moments, and mutual support. For them, having a friend is (or should be) like having a superfan, so it ends up not being fair at all for the victim.

You might want to save your friend from their inflated self-esteem and the ways it affects their life, but just like in a romantic relationship, your friend has to want to change in order for you to successfully support them. If you see no effort from their part, it is time for you to go your own way and focus on your healthy friendships with trustworthy people who fill your life with laughter and fun times.

A Narcissistic Friendship: An Example

Paul and Marc met at the park while they were walking their dogs. They seemed to have a lot in common from their conversations at the park, so they decided they should go get a beer one day. They did, and after a while, they became good friends. Marc always made Paul laugh with his stories, and they had fun.

But alas, things started to change. Paul became so close to Marc that Marc saw the perfect opportunity to get his newest supply. Once, Paul decided to go walk his dog with another friend, Frank, and he posted a photo of them on his social media profile. As soon as Paul saw Marc again, the narcissist did not take long to start bad-mouthing Frank. "He used to have a drug problem, you know? Do you really want to associate with someone like that? I really don't think you should."

This became a pattern with anyone Paul chose to hang out with until one day he decided to say something about it. He confronted Marc and asked him why he felt the need to talk trash about anyone that he was friends with. He could not have predicted Marc's reaction as he aggressively yelled at him that he only wanted to protect him from bad people and accused him of not being grateful of the only true friend he had. Marc found a way of putting the blame on Paul even though he did nothing wrong.

Marc's notion of friendship was not healthy, and that showed in his connection with Paul. His need for constant attention made Paul not enjoy spending time with him anymore, as is usual with any narcissistic friend.

Narcissism at Work

The last type of relationship I will cover is one that can be extremely frustrating even though you only see this person for a certain number of hours a day. I'm talking about work relationships. Some people you meet throughout your career become your friends outside the office while others you would rather not see anywhere else than that office. The narcissists in your workplace probably fit in the second category, but even those 40 hours a week (or less) that you have to deal with them might sometimes seem like a lifetime.

The big reason why it is so disheartening if the narcissist in your life is someone you work with is that you (hopefully) started working there to be successful, and just imagining the journey to get there was something that got you truly excited. That alone can be a challenge, and having another person come in your way and become an extra obstacle is never fun.

The people whose narcissism will affect you the most are those who work with you more closely, and they can be your coworkers or your boss. Each can have different consequences on your performance at work because of how they relate to you in terms of the company hierarchy.

Signs Your Colleague Is Narcissistic

Once again, the person's narcissism will start to show up over time. Because the work time is such a specific occasion, the signs will also be quite specific, which is good news for you because it allows you to pinpoint more easily who the narcissist in your life is. So when you are at the office, look at your colleagues and check if they continuously do any of the following.

- **They claim your ideas as theirs.** As coworkers, teamwork will be an important part of your job. This means sharing thoughts and ideas, which may put you in a disfavorable situation, especially if the two of you do the brainstorming by yourselves. No one will really be able to know who had the idea, so they will not have a reason to believe that your colleague is basically stealing your idea.

- **They don't accept feedback on their work.** Just like brainstorming, giving and receiving feedback is a huge part of working in a team. For a narcissist, though, the receiving part is not necessary as mistakes are never their fault. Whatever you are about to say regarding their work is not actually true; it is simply an attack to them as a person. They think you are making things up because you are jealous of how well they are doing at their job.

- **They believe they should be in a position of leadership**, and they know how to manipulate others into thinking the same. A study conducted in 2008 by the Sage Journal proved that there is a direct connection between narcissistic traits and leader emergence, which explains why they often end up in authority roles even if they don't meet the necessary requirements (Sage Journal, 2008).

- **They see themselves as a VIP in the company** right from the start and will name-drop at any moment to prove that, whether it is the college they studied at, the company they worked at before, the references they have in their résumé—anything to prove that they are better than you.

- Although they love showing off their (fake) skills

and telling everyone how talented they are, how they were born to do that exact job, and how they should definitely be the next boss in the company or department, **when it is time to actually do the work, they are rarely ever one of the best at it**. That is why they feel the need to take credit for their colleagues' ideas and work.

- **They have no problem suggesting unethical work practices** to you if that will get you two to the goal faster. The only thing that matters to them is having results to show to the boss and not how you get to those results because, in his mind, you two can always lie about it and make your teamwork look good anyway.

How Working with a Narcissistic Colleague Affects Your Performance at Work

All these behaviors combined are bound to create a toxic environment in the office, which is very disappointing, especially if you were excited about this job and it is exactly what you have always dreamed of doing career-wise. It can be so powerful that it sucks the fun out of the role and makes you feel nothing but exhaustion. It can damage your motivation and make you feel like you will never achieve the goals you established as long as you keep working with the person. At first, you try to fight this person's behavior, but you quickly realize that it will not be as easy as you initially thought, and you might even start questioning if it is worth it, or if you should simply go with the flow and let them be as dominant as they wish to be.

Your job is supposed to make you feel fulfilled and excited, and when you find the one you are actually passionate about, that you gladly spend 40 hours every week for, it is crazy to think that just one person can show up and ruin that.

However, there are ways to deal with a narcissistic coworker and not let them win, which you will get to know in the fifth chapter. For now, let's see a practical example of this kind of relationship.

Working with a Narcissist: An Example

Susie works at a model agency as a photographer. Her role involves not only taking the pictures but also coming up with creative settings and ideas for shoots according to the briefings passed on by the clients. She had known she wanted to work in photography ever since she was a kid, and her dad bought her a disposable camera. The love for that art form was instant!

Susie was doing the job on her own up to that point, but because the company was growing at a fast pace and they kept getting more and more clients, they decided it was time for Susie to get a fellow photographer. So they hired Brock.

Brock's views on photography were different than Susie's, as he kind of just ended up becoming a photographer. However, despite the lack of passion, Brock got into the set on the first day with the clear intention of becoming Susie's boss and, eventually, go up on the hierarchy until he reached the highest position.

The first project that Susie and Brock worked together on was a photoshoot for a skater clothing brand. They got the request from the client, and it was time to brainstorm, so they went to a small meetings room and discussed ideas. Susie came up with a great general idea, which they both developed into the final concept for the shoot that they were going to present to the boss and the client on the next day.

The following day came, and it was time to inform the boss of the creative path they chose for the photoshoot. To Susie's surprised, Brock ended up taking complete credit of the idea. She was expecting his sentence to start with a "we," but instead, it started with an "I."

Susie felt really frustrated and tried to talk to Brock, asking him never to do that again. He took great offense to what she was accusing him of and told her that he participated as well. In fact, he felt like most of the concept came from his ideas, and for that reason, he believed he should be the one taking credit for it.

More projects came, and Brock maintained that attitude that Susie could not deal with. Brock wanted so badly to show the boss that he was the best while actually not doing half of the job that he should. During the first few times, Susie continued trying to make people understand that he was not as talented as he showed and that he was instead a big liar, but she was always unsuccessfully.

With time, Susie's motivation started fading away. The job that she was so passionate about became an obligation. She was longing for those sweet 48 hours of the weekend from the moment she stepped in on the office on Monday morning. Susie's dream job did not make her happy anymore, and her coworker's narcissism was to blame.

Signs Your Boss Is Narcissistic

Remember how much I talked about leaders in the first

chapter, where we explained the concept of narcissism? I mostly focused on world leaders and people who are globally known, but your narcissistic boss is like a version of them at a much lower level. Your boss has reached the narcissistic peak (getting to a position of authority), and they will enjoy it to the fullest. So if you read the following red flags and recognize your boss in them, you might just be getting mentorship from someone who suffers from acute narcissism.

- **They don't really like to give you credit for your good work.** In fact, just like the narcissistic coworker, the narcissistic boss might even steal your ideas and present them as theirs. The only occasion when they will give you credit is when they need or want something from you. Apart from that, you (and the other employees) are completely replaceable; thus, you are not worthy of their appraisal.

- They exploit you, meaning that **they make you do a lot more than what your job title entails**, particularly in the scope of the narcissistic manager's personal life. So they would put on you things like walking their dog or going to get a personal order. Furthermore, it is not uncommon for the manager to ask you to do something that is a part of their own responsibilities without giving you proper credit in the end.

- **They don't show any empathy for their employees' feelings or problems.** No one is in their A-game every single day. Maybe something happened to your personal life, or maybe you are sick, or maybe you are just having a bad day for no apparent reason. All of those come with being a human being, and an empathetic boss would understand that is not easy to separate personal life/health from work and would try to help you so that you can feel better as soon as possible and go back to being the productive employee you usually are. But that is not the case with a narcissistic boss. Instead, they would let you know that none of that matters once you step inside the office and that you should be able to deal with your issues by yourself.

- **They want to control everything and everyone**, and their favorite means to do so is by using fear and making threats. They make it very clear that whoever messes up is in huge trouble because they are not afraid of using their power to make sure everyone stays in their lane even if that lane is outside the office.

- They are very competitive, and **they also instill an environment of rivalry between their employees** by constantly comparing them to one another, consequently making them want to surpass their colleagues instead of focusing on simply doing their job well and as a team.

How Having a Narcissistic Boss Affects Your Performance at Work

Equally to having a narcissistic coworker, having a narcissistic boss has the potential to destroy the love and passion you feel for your job. And in this case, it might be even worse because according to the company's hierarchy, this person is in a higher position than you, so they have power over you. This might make it harder for you to confront them when they abuse that power, especially if this is your first job or if you just don't deal well with confrontation, let alone with someone in a position of authority.

Having a manager who repeatedly puts you down and is incapable of appreciating your good work can severely damage your self-esteem and make you run away from a career that would otherwise allow you to live the professional life of your dreams, which is utterly unfair.

Having a Narcissistic Boss: An Example

Coby is a recent graduate in advertising, and after his well-deserved summer travelings, he got an internship at a well-known ad agency. His manager is Francis, a lady in her thirties who had been working in the agency for about five years and who, to be fair, seemed quite nice to Coby on their first interview.

Coby had always been a creative person. In college, he discovered his passion and effortless skills for copywriting, so getting this job could not be more exciting to him. He had always heard that being an intern meant getting coffees and organizing boring paperwork, so he was mentally prepared to take on that kind of tasks. However, he could not have predicted and mentally prepare himself for how draining working for Francis would be.

The coffees had to be taken, the dogs had to be walked, the paperwork had to be cataloged daily, the fish had to be fed, and at least once a week, the new dress or heels she ordered had to be picked up from the post office. On top of all that, not only did he have his copywriting tasks, but Francis would constantly pass on to him management tasks that should be handled by her.

Coby was always exhausted, and that started to take a toll on his mental health and his social life as he got work burnout and barely had time to see his friends and family anymore. And never did he get a "Thank you" or "Good job."

By the end of the internship, Coby decided to confront Francis and let her know that he did not think her attitude was fair, but she was quick to tell him that she could easily find someone to do the same job that he did, and probably better, and that once his internship was over, he was fired.

As a result of his manager's narcissism, Coby had an awful first experience working in the area that he loved the most, and that ended up having a big impact on his personal life as well.

Step 3: A Summary

1. If you are in a relationship and feel like your partner does not treat and appreciate you the way that they should, **observe their behavior in your romantic partnership**. Do they ignore your feelings, blame you for everything bad that happens to you two, try to force their beliefs and values on you, make you turn your back on your loved ones, and verbally and/or physically abuse you?

2. In case **you feel like the narcissist in your life is a relative, notice how your relationship has evolved**. This relative could be of any degree, but parents and siblings are the ones who would affect you the most. If you believe your mother or your father was a narcissist, recall your childhood and how it may have been different than usual. Did they force you to keep your emotions to yourself and try to turn you into their "mini-me" without taking into consideration the person who you wanted to be? Did they never show you the love and support that every kid should receive?

If you suspect it is your brother or sister, have they always been extremely competitive with you? Did they try to paint a negative image of you to your other family members while manipulating and mistreating you on their backs? Were they jealous of any victory you had in your life?

3. The one other family member who can greatly affect your life with their narcissism is your child. However, in this case, you should keep in mind that a lot a child's narcissism comes from the way they are brought up, so more than trying to change them, you should analyze your behavior as well as your partner's behavior and what you two might be doing to feed the kid's ego in such an unhealthy manner. **A narcissistic child is still a narcissist in the making, so take the time you have now to change the way their personality is developing** and turn them into a healthy grown up.

4. **Friends are often said to be the family you get to choose, so having a narcissistic one can be just as heartbreaking.** If you have a feeling that one of your friends is the narcissist in your life, once again, observing the

relationship between you two and remembering how it started versus how it is now will give you a better idea if your suspicions are real or not. Is this friend unable to give you support and advice? Do they talk trash about people you both know, and have you started feeling uneasy every time you two hang out?

5. **And finally, the narcissist in your life might be someone you work with.** If one of your coworkers constantly steals your ideas, suggests unethical ways for you two to achieve the proposed goals, and exaggerates their skills, they might be a narcissist. If your boss never gives you praise for your good work, puts way too many (unsuitable) tasks on you, and uses fear to maintain order, then they might be the ones with an inflated ego.

100% FREE Ebook!

LEARN HOW YOU CAN ENJOY YOUR GADGETS WITHOUT LOSING YOUR ABILITY TO COMMUNICATE IN REAL LIFE!

Claim Your Free Copy Now!
https://maxjharrison.com/moderntechnology

Step 4: Understand Common Triggers of NPD

The triggers to one's narcissism are the situations and circumstances that usually lead them to react in a narcissistic way. Narcissistic personality disorder is a mental condition, so although a person who suffers from it is a narcissist all the time, they only overreact at certain events. These overreactions usually take the form of angry outbursts, public humiliation of others, passive-aggressiveness, and mental and/or verbal abuse; and they exist as a form of defense to a situation that feels like a threat.

Each person with a narcissistic personality disorder is unique, but there are some patterns as to what tends to trigger them into narcissistic frenzies. The following situations are typical threats to the narcissist:

- **When they are ignored.** Narcissists have a constant need for attention, so when you stop giving it to them, especially if you had been a regular supply up until that point, that will trigger them.

- **When they are asked questions that they don't know how to answer or to carry out tasks that they cannot handle.** Narcissists want to project an image of someone who is good at anything and everything, and when you ask something from them that they don't know how to do, you ruin that image of perfection.

- **When people they consider to be below them don't treat them with superiority.** Narcissists have interiorized that they deserve special treatment and that only very few people are on their level. So not meeting the exaggerated, unrealistic standards that the narcissists established constitutes a trigger.

- **When someone who has a different point of view on something tries to discuss it with them**, even if in a polite, constructive manner. The narcissist's perspective is the only one that is valuable in their mind, so trying to challenge it feels like an attack instead of a learning opportunity.

- **When someone they are close to does better than them.** Narcissists are jealous by nature. They want to be on top, and when someone threatens their chances, they don't know how to have a healthy reaction, like congratulating the person and trying to take some tips from them.

- **When someone they are close to tries to have an emotional conversation** that would need them to be more vulnerable than they are comfortable with. Staying completely out of touch with their emotions is a golden rule for narcissists, so when someone tries to talk about their feelings, it can be very distressing for the narcissist.

- **When someone tells them "no."** Narcissists want everything their way, and they want it now. Refusing to do what a narcissist tells you to feels to them like you are questioning their superiority and power.

- **If someone they know is self-confident in a healthy way** and can conduct themselves with poise while achieving the goals they set themselves up to achieve. Basically, people who are able to do this are the type of people narcissist want to be, so it feels threatening to them and to their own success.

- **When they know, deep down, that they**

made a mistake. Never assuming guilt is another one of a narcissist's gold rules even if they were the ones who messed up. We know by now that they lie and manipulate to make themselves look good, but being aware of their own mistakes is like a confirmation of the self-esteem issues they have that they mask with the narcissism.

- **When someone tries to give them advice.** A narcissist is always in control, and they never need help. Trying to give them a piece of advice or opinion is like doubting that they have the skills to do whatever they have to do, which, again, feels like a personal attack to them.

As you read the list of possible triggers, it is possible that you felt like you were reading about a child. It is an understandable comparison because narcissists are very emotionally and psychologically immature. These triggers result in what we can compare to a tantrum thrown by a child, but in this case, they are thrown by an adult. The reason behind every single one of the triggers is simple: fear. People with NPD are afraid of any situation that might reveal to the world that they are not perfect and that they don't have it all figured out. In fact, in 1984, Rothstein, in his study *Fear of Humiliation*, referred to a direct link between the loss of perfection and the feeling of humiliation with the development of a narcissistic personality (NCBI, 2013). In 1999, Kernberg, in his case report called "A Severe Sexual Inhibition in the Course of the Psychoanalytic Treatment of a Patient with a Narcissistic Personality Disorder," mentioned the exploration of hidden fears as a way of treating narcissistic personality disorder (NCBI, 2013).

Is Aging a Trigger to the Worsening of NPD?

Narcissistic or not, as a person gets older, they stop caring as much in general. We have all heard that from our grandparents. So what happens when someone with narcissistic personality disorder gets old? What does this more carefree attitude mean for them?

One study conducted in 2018 observed a sample of 200 participants, half of them of middle age (35 to 55) and the other half of older age (65 to 85). The objective was to understand the link between the loneliness that might come with aging and the levels of narcissism. For that, they measured the participants' loneliness levels through the 20-item UCLA Loneliness Scale (Version

3), the participants' narcissism levels through the 40-item Narcissistic Personality Inventory, and their cognitive assessment through the Mini-Bog Test. In the end, they concluded that narcissism was lower in people with older age (but loneliness was higher) (NCBI, 2018).

Another study carried out by Daniel Segal, Victor Molinari, and Richard Zweig in 2012 that focused on what happened with personality disorders as people got older also referenced the narcissistic personality disorder. The authors state that with age, people with NPD get a better ability to deal with consequences of their disorder, therefore being able to manage their symptoms.

It seems like there is a negative correlation between age and narcissism, but alas, it is not that simple because there is a research study done in May of 2011 that shows different conclusions. One single 85-year-old divorced woman was the object of the study for three separate meetings that happened within the period of two months. On said meetings, the lady was asked to analyze the effects of aging on her from her current point of view, as well as from the point of view of her younger self. The study suggested that as people with NPD get older, they may have a hard time with the physical and psychological changes that will inevitably happen, and they react to them as if they are a threat instead of in an accepting way as a healthy person would. So even if her NPD symptoms diminished, the way that she looked at the process of aging and its effects on her was still with the eyes of a narcissist.

Of course, studying a sample of 200 people or the specific case of one single individual is completely different, but it goes to show that every narcissist is unique. So the answer to the question posed on the title of this subchapter is that there is no definite conclusion, but there is definitely hope that, with age, narcissism starts to mitigate.

How to Deal with Your Triggers

The easiest way of understanding how you can challenge your narcissistic personality disorder is by breaking down the process step by step, so that is what we will do in this subchapter. But firstly, it is important for you to know that changing any personality disorder is a big challenge and requires real effort. I have talked before about the possibility of being followed by a therapist, which is something you can definitely combine with this step-by-step recovery process.

However, as much time and effort as it might require from you, in the end, the results are always worth it. So before you even start reading the step-to-step guide on how to change your narcissistic behavior, you need to get in the right mindset. It is not only okay but also actually amazing to want to improve!

Step 1: Identify what triggers your narcissistic reactions

You cannot deal with your triggers if you are not aware of what they are, so that is precisely what the first step is all about: awareness. They might be some of the ones I listed or others that are completely different. You will need to do some self-analysis and observe your own demeanor in order to understand what makes you react with exaggerated rage or with rude passive-aggressiveness.

So what you do for this first step is writing down specific situations in your daily life that triggered you to respond in a narcissistic manner. You can write down on a notebook or simply put them on the notes on your phone. Do this for a couple of weeks, and after a while, you will probably see a pattern on the situations that you compiled so you will have a better awareness of what kind of events lead you to these unwanted responses.

Step 2: Identify the mischievous behaviors that those triggers usually lead to and that you want to change

Now that you know what leads you to respond in a narcissistic manner, it is time to assess what that actually means. So the observation exercises continue. What are your typical reactions to triggering events? Usually, narcissists have one of two types of reaction: either an angry one or a passive-aggressive one.

So do you lash out at people, either verbally or physically, when they do something that threatens you? Do you get violent with yourself and self-harm to release the anger you feel? Do you passively try to manipulate the people who put you in a triggering situation?

So in that same notebook (or notes on your phone) where you wrote down your triggers, write down your typical behaviors.

Step 3: Try to come up with healthier ways of reacting to the triggers

Steps 1 and 2 focused a lot on the negatives, but step 3 is when that changes. From now on, the focal point will be on turning this harmful situation into a positive, healthy way of living.

The time to observe has ended, and it is now time to analyze and reflect. For this step, you will need to have some free time on your hands. Go to a place where you feel safe and comfortable and get the notebook where you wrote down your triggers and narcissistic behaviors. For each of those behaviors, ask yourself, "How can I change this response and make it more balanced?"

In your ideal life, how would you deal with adversities? Write that down next to each negative response from step 2.

Step 4: Practice managing your narcissistic responses and avoiding impulsiveness

We have observed, and we have analyzed. Now it is time to start doing. The fourth step will require from you a level of self-control that you probably don't know you are even able to achieve. Up until this point, impulsiveness ruled your reactions. According to the psychiatrist Adam Blatner, a healthy person normally goes through seven stages of anger: stress, anxiety, agitation, irritation, frustration, anger, and lastly, rage. Someone with NPD, however, is typically very quick to jump automatically to the last stage, which is rage. Your goal with the fourth step is to start incorporating more stages into your own anger process so that you don't lose your temper at the smallest trigger you encounter.

Note that the goal is *not* for you to bottle up your feelings of anger but to learn how to deal with them in a healthy way. Anger is a natural emotion that every single human being feels from time to time, and suppressing it would do more damage than good.

There are several techniques you can adopt to avoid impulsive reactions, and you will probably need to try a few in order to understand what works best for you. I will give you three anger management exercises you can start with in your recovery process:

Do breathing exercises. Every time you start feeling the rage building up inside of you, you can force yourself to do a series of breathing exercises. One example is deep breathing:

1. Breathe in deeply through your nose.

2. Then breathe out, also through your nose.

3. Put one hand on your stomach and the other one on your chest so that you can feel the movement of your body as you breathe in and out.

4. Repeat step 1 and step 2 three or four more times and focus on the movement of your belly

and chest as you do it.

You might feel like this would never be enough to control you in moments when you feel angry, but it is a fact that the anger you feel is a consequence of your brain letting the rest of your body know that you are in a situation of emergency. So you start feeling your heartbeat go faster, as well as your breathing cycles, because your body goes into survival mode. Doing some breathing exercises lets your body know that it is not, in fact, going through a crisis, so there is no need to go into fight-or-flight mode just yet. It is a great way of telling your brain to relax and to be able to think of ways of reacting that are not as rageful as they would normally be.

Count to ten before you react. This simple tip works because of an also simple reason: it gives you time to think. You can apply it any time, anywhere, with anyone, so there is no real excuse not to at least give it a go. When you give yourself time to process what just happened, you also give your rational side some time to meet your emotional side, which can result in more balanced, reasonable responses. You distract your brain from the rage, and when you remember what happened again, you don't feel such intense emotions.

Find a song that makes you feel calm and have it on your phone. Your senses can be really powerful, as can be music and its impact on you. We all have songs that make us feel a certain way, and if you don't have one already, you need to find a song that fills you with good and calm energies. Have it downloaded on your phone so that you don't need internet access to listen to it. When you start to feel your brain going a thousand miles a minute and the stress and anger taking over, put your headphones on and do nothing but listen to the song you chose. Let the good feelings replace the negatives ones you were starting to feel. You can even complement this technique with the deep breathing exercises for more potent outcomes.

Step 5: Practice applying the healthy responses you came up with on step 3

Once you have calmed yourself down and distanced yourself from the situation for a little bit, it is easier for you to consciously apply the healthier responses you have written down on your notebook before. You can repeatedly play situations in your mind where you replace the toxic behavior with a positive one, or you can even ask your therapist to do some role-playing exercises where you can practice this (if they have not suggested that already).

Step 6: Analyze the results of the changes you applied (and celebrate even the tiniest victory!)

Thrivingly changing behaviors that you have had for your entire life is not something that will happen overnight or that you will figure out at the first attempt. There will probably be some adjustments needed to your approach and some error and trial until you get a grasp of what works best for you.

Your narcissism might make you feel defeated and like pretending is easier than actually doing the work and changing your ways, but after a while, you will see some progress, and that will be good not only to yourself but also to the people who love and care about you.

A Step-by-Step NPD Recovery Plan in Action

So what does this plan look like in action? Let's take a look at Felicia, a woman in her twenties who is part of a group of friends that she met in college. Felicia is aware that she does not react the best way when things don't go the way she wants, and that has caused her to start being excluded from the group's plans. Deep down, Felicia knows she is in the wrong, and she wants to change so that she can keep her friends and start doing fun things with them again. So she applies the six steps to recovery.

Step 1: Felicia observes her own behavior with her friends and realizes that her trigger is when they try to prove a point that goes against what she believes. Felicia has always been a bit of a know-it-all, and although that was cute when she was a young girl, now that she is becoming an adult, she is starting to feel the negative impacts of such demeanor.

Step 2: Felicia comes to a conclusion that, in those triggering situations, she becomes very passive-aggressive. She is unable to listen to her friends and is clearly bothered by what is happening, yet when her friends try to get to talk about what she is feeling, she always says that everything is fine and she is not mad. This makes it very difficult for her friends to connect with her and try to approach her in a different way that is not as triggering for her, so after a while, they start to give up on trying.

Step 3: Felicia plays those situations in her mind and understands that the way she would like to respond to them would be by having a healthy discussion with her friends, gracefully accepting the cases where she was in the wrong. She wants to see this kind of conversations as an opportunity to learn about the topic being discussed and/or about her friends' points of view without thinking that they are attacking her or threatening her intelligence.

Step 4: Felicia does some research on techniques to calm herself down in situations of narcissistic rage, and after trying a couple, she realizes that what relaxes her the most is doing some deep breathing exercises while holding a necklace that her mother once gave her without the knowledge of her narcissistic father. So she practices the exercises and starts carrying the necklace everywhere.

Step 5: After letting her friends know that she is working on her attitude problems, they invite her to go have lunch with them. During the lunch, one of her friends says he disagrees with her on something, and that causes some anger to start building up inside Felicia. When she notices she is going down the wrong path again, she holds her necklace and does one series of breathing exercises. After that, she is able to defend her argument in a healthy way, and in the end, her friends come to a conclusion that Felicia is in fact right. The entire group likes Felicia's change in the way she responded. Over time, as they see that she is truly committed to getting better, they start including her in more and more of their plans.

Step 6: In the previous situation with her friends, Felicia does very good, and she feels quite proud of herself. However, she notices that, a couple of days later, when a disagreement happens with an acquaintance, she does not put her recovery plan into practice. She comes to the conclusion that, because it is not someone whom she cares much about and even knows that well, she does not think to be more careful with her response. However, she wants to be able to have healthy discussions with anyone, no matter how close they are, so she concludes that being able to calm down when speaking to acquaintances or strangers is something she still needs to work on.

Step 4: A Summary

1. Understand the common triggers that people with narcissistic personality disorder usually struggle with. Do any of those make you respond in a negative way?

2. If you realize that you have triggers to your narcissism, what are the negative responses that you tend to go for, and what do you think would be better ways of handling such situations?

3. Practice those healthier reactions, either in your mind, with a therapist, or with a loved one whom you can ask for support. Practice makes

perfect, especially when it comes to rewiring your brain.

4. Start putting your new reactions in practice in real-life situations. Don't lose motivation if you find this step to be very difficult. Doing this successfully, to the point where it becomes natural to you, will take a long time. You are telling your brain to do the complete opposite of what it is used to, and changing habits never happens overnight.

5. Continue to work on your recovery, and if you realize that you need to change your approach, do it. Changing your plan does not equal failing but being aware of your inevitable imperfections and showing commitment to the process. And don't forget to celebrate your victories!

Step 5: Understand How You Can Deal with the Narcissist in Your Life

Now you know what you can do if the narcissist in your life is yourself. But what if it is someone else? What can you do to protect yourself from becoming a supply? How can you escape from a narcissist after you have fallen into their trap? And also, how can you help someone who wants to fight their narcissistic personality disorder?

The answers to these questions will depend on each case, but there are some guidelines you can follow according to the type of relationship you have with the narcissist. Like I did in the third chapter, I will cover four kinds of connections: romantic relationships, family relationship, friendships, and work relationships. I will also do a follow-up on each example I gave on that chapter, showing how the narcissist's loved ones on each case could deal with them.

How Can I Deal with My Narcissist Partner?

This can be a tricky question to answer, especially now that you know how manipulative narcissists can be and how much they are willing to lie and deceive for their own enjoyment and satisfaction. However, and as has been said, not all narcissists are horrible people, and the one you fell in love with might actually want to change for the better.

When Your Partner Is Abusive

The first thing that should be said on this topic is that you cannot change someone unless they want to. If your partner does not show any signs that they want to put in effort into bettering how they act in the relationship and in their life in general, there is no point in you even trying. Also, if they have ever been physically abusive toward you, there is no guarantee that they will not do it again. So if you find yourself in one of those situations, pack your bags and go. It is easier said than done, but you are a valuable person who does not deserve to endure any type of abuse and who needs to understand their own value before you even think about trying to fix someone who does not want to be fixed.

It can also happen that your partner has moments when they tell you that they are ready to work for your future together and to make it work in a healthy way but then are quick to go back to their narcissistic, controlling, angry self. If that is the situation you are currently in, try to break the cycle. As soon as you feel that one second of unbreakable courage to walk out that door and never look back, go. Here are some tips for you to escape your abusive partner:

While you are still living with them, **make a copy of your important documents**. They might hide it as a way of blackmailing you, so having the copies will give you an advantage. Be sure to only make the copies when your partner is not at home so that you don't raise any suspicions.

Don't tell them that you are leaving them. Just take the first chance you have without them seeing, and go. If you let them know, they will do whatever they can to make you stay, and they will probably punish you for even thinking of abandoning them.

Contact a friend or family member to help you. At this point, you are probably not very close to your loved ones anymore and letting them know that they were right by not liking your partner might be hard to do. However, as you leave these horrible circumstances behind, you also leave your life behind, so you need to have somewhere to go. If you tell someone you were once close with about the situation you are in, chances are, they will help you. After all, they don't want you to suffer, and they will be happy and proud that you are finally letting go of the toxic person in your life.

Become uncontactable to the narcissist. This means changing your phone number and e-mail address, as well as deleting your social media accounts and creating new ones with a different name. You have to become invisible to your abuser. Also, while you are still living with them, take any chance you can to make sure you are not logged into any of your social media accounts on their devices.

If the narcissist manages to find out where you are or how to contact you, **don't believe anything they say to try to convince you to get back together with them**. When someone purposely and repeatedly hurts, whether it is physically or psychologically, there should be no giving them one more chance. If your partner gets a hold of you, they will do anything they can to try to get their supply (i.e., you) back, and most of what they say will be nothing more than lies. Stay strong and away.

Report your situation to the authorities or even just to a therapist. This can be scary and nerve-wracking, but verbal and physical abuse should never go unseen and unpunished. It will leave scars on you forever, and once your partner decides to give up on trying to get you back, they will simply play the same mind games with another person and abuse them instead. Does not sound that fair, does it? Get a friend to go with you to the police or the doctor, and get everything on record.

If your partner is not willing to spend money and time on professional help, their narcissistic ways will not magically change, so even if they try to convince you that, if they want to, they can get better by themselves, you cannot believe that. And if they are abusive toward you, staying with them should never even be an option. Your safety needs to come first!

How to Heal from an Abusive Relationship with a Narcissist

Now that you are finally out of that awful situation, not only is it time to make sure you stay away, but it is also time for you to heal. Healing is different for everyone in the methods that work, how long it takes, and what it is deep inside that needs healing. Anyone who goes through a break up needs to heal their broken heart. In cases like this, the abuse takes the healing process to an entirely new level because it is such a traumatic event.

Victims need to take time to take care of themselves and either go back to being or become for the first time a happy, independent individual who sees their worth and can stand up for themselves. Otherwise, the wounds left from the relationship will become bigger and deeper, and that can result in serious mental issues. Below are some healing techniques for people who got out of an abusive, narcissistic relationship are:

- **Don't blame yourself for falling in love with this person or for the way they treated you.** For good and for bad, love is something you cannot control. When you first met this person and you started feeling the butterflies and all the good things, you couldn't have predicted that they would end up treating you the way they did. The abuser always existed within them, way before they met you. You were simply (and unfortunately) their means to unleashing all the anger that they had been feeling for so long. Nothing about the situation was your fault.

- **Allow yourself to feel angry and sad**

about the abuse. Anger, sadness, disappointment—these are all natural emotions that every single one of us has felt before. Being mistreated by someone who was supposed to love and protect you is awful, so if you feel negative emotions, let them out. Bottling them up will end up hurting you even more in the long run. So if you need to let go of negative emotions, start doing CrossFit, write down what is going through your mind, or just break a couple of glasses. Do anything that works for you and that allows you to put those emotions on the outside. With time, you will accept what happened to you, become at peace with it, and be able to move on as an even stronger person.

- **Work on loving yourself and on feeling powerful again.** An abusive relationship can completely shatter the victim's self-love. You hear and feel on your own skin how unworthy you are, so you start to believe it. But in reality, it is not true. You were a victim to the abuse when it was going on, but you have been a survivor from the start. Rediscover yourself and don't close yourself off from your loved ones. It is essential that you tell yourself how worthy of love you are so that you can rebuild the relationships that were harmed by the toxic partner and accept with open arms new ones that are to come.

- **Tell yourself positive, healing affirmations every day.** It might seem like it will not do much, but talking to yourself on a positive note every single day can do wonders to your mindset, especially if you do it right when you wake up as a way of setting the tone for the rest of the day. Remember how hearing your partner telling you every day how useless you are made you start believing it? The logic is the same, but the end results are the complete opposite. For whatever is troubling you, find a positive sentence (or more—as many as you need, really) that challenges that. If you are constantly doubting yourself, tell yourself, "Today I will trust myself to make good, healthy decisions." If you don't believe you are worthy of other people's affection, tell yourself, "I will accept and be grateful for the love other people give me because I deserve it." And so on!

- **If you feel like it is all getting a little bit too much, seek professional help.** Dealing with such trauma and getting over it all by yourself is very hard, and even with the support of family and friends, it can be challenging. Some therapists specialize in helping people who have been victims of verbal and/or physical abuse by their spouse, so if you ever feel like you will not be able to heal by yourself, know that there are people out there who are professionally certified to help people who have been through the same experiences as you.

When Your Partner Wants to Change

If this person (who has *never* been physically or verbally abusive toward you) goes to you looking for support as they start going to therapy or attending support groups, you can consider giving them support.

As you give the other person aid in their recovery, it is important that you read about what narcissism (or better yet, NPD) truly is and get information that goes further than the basic notion of narcissism that you probably have at this point. Maybe that is why you are reading this book, and if you have gotten to this stage of your relationship with a narcissist, I salute you. As you learn more about the condition, you will understand that if you want to continue being a couple and try to fix the relationship as a team or if you want to put a boundary on your relationship and tell them that you will be there for them but solely as a friend, it is crucial that you listen to your own feelings so that you don't end up staying with someone because you feel sorry for them and don't want to hurt them. You will not be able to support the narcissist if you are not happy and healthy.

Here are some tips on how to deal with your narcissistic partner:

- Slowly, **start decreasing the amount of attention** that you give them. If you are still at the beginning of the relationship, you haven't gotten them used to a certain amount of attention, so don't set their expectations high. Make them understand that you have more things to do than giving them your full attention. Set boundaries as to what they can expect from you and stay firm.

- **When you two are discussing and your partner starts feeling angry or defensive, try to assess if it is worth fighting over that topic.** But if it something that truly matters, tell your partner to do the calming exercise they have been practicing so that you can continue talking without it getting out control.

- When they start setting unrealistic goals, **calmly tell them that you think it would be best if you established results that are a little bit more prudent**. Explain to them step by step and in an objective way why doing so would be more beneficial for them. Hit them with facts and not so much with feelings.

- **Try to understand where this behavior comes from.** Maybe their parents abused them when they were kids, or maybe they were never shown any care and warmth during their childhood. The narcissist will not open up easily, but with time and therapy, you might start getting to know a side of them that was a huge secret. Be careful not to push the person too hard as they might have a lot of underlying trauma.

- **Help your partner find a therapist and try to get them to communicate** with you throughout their recovery, as well as triggers they usually come across, so that you can do what's within your reach to minimize those triggers or help them deal with them. You can see, if you go on a session with the therapist, where the three of you can focus on the relationship and what is needed from both parts to make it work. Make sure that your partner is putting in the effort and it is not just you who is trying to adjust to their narcissistic demeanor.

- **Congratulate them on their successes.** What your partner is going through is not easy. Recovery is a tough process, no matter what the condition being treated is. Specific positive reinforcement is great to fight the self-esteem problem the narcissist has without feeding the huge ego that is being used as a mask.

- You can **give couples' therapy a try**, but keep in mind that, in order to be effective, both people in the relationship need to participate. So even if you strongly believe that the sessions would be beneficial for you two, if your partner is not ready for such type of therapy, maybe it is not time to take that approach just yet.

The important thing here is that you put your own safety and happiness before theirs. They need to get better. It is always good to praise when someone admits they have a problem and reaches out for help, but if this relationship has been damaging to you and your own mental state, you cannot underestimate that.

Put yourself first and then help your partner.

Dealing with a Narcissistic Partner: Michael and Stephanie's Story

In the example I mentioned in chapter 3, Michael met Stephanie, a narcissist, and ended up falling madly in love with her. The two got married, and a couple of months into the engagement, Stephanie started to show her narcissistic personality. When Michael tried to confront her about it, Stephanie got really angry and asked for a divorce.

Let's say that Stephanie has some time to reflect and decides she wants to learn how to deal with her triggers so that she and Michael can be together and happy. After carefully thinking about his own feelings and happiness, Michael realizes that he still loves Stephanie, so he decides to give her another chance, so long as she actually works on improving her attitude and that she understands that he has other relationships that he needs to maintain and care for, namely with friends and family, so she cannot expect him to be with her 24/7.

Stephanie goes to therapy every week, and a few sessions in, she decides to open up to Michael. She lets him know that her father was very harsh on her when she was a child and that such treatment coming from who was supposed to be her hero really damaged the way she functioned. She tells him about what triggers her to respond aggressively and asks to practice with him some techniques that her therapist has taught her.

Michael is really happy that his girlfriend is finally honest with him, but he knows that her childhood is a touchy subject, so he navigates through the conversation with caution, never asking too many questions and quickly changing topics when Stephanie seems to be getting too uncomfortable. After this moment, it is impossible for Michael to refuse to help her with her exercises. In fact, for a couple of weeks, Michael and Stephanie practice the exercises every other day and talk about her progress. It is not always easy, and sometimes Stephanie still lashes out when she is in triggering situations. However, with time, Stephanie becomes more and more comfortable with emotional conversations with her partner, and her violent responses start happening way less often.

Stephanie knows she could not have gotten that far without the support of her boyfriend, and now they live a happy life together.

Tips to Deal with a Narcissist Family Member

With Your Narcissistic Parent

When the narcissist in your life is your mother or your father, you are in one of three situations: (1) you still live under one roof and depend on them, (2) you have moved out but still want to try to keep some kind of relationship, or (3) you have moved out and decided to cut ties with your narcissistic parent.

If you are in the third situation, you have already found a way of handling the narcissist in your life. However, if you are in one of the first two, you need to learn how to deal with them in a way that does not destroy your self-esteem and self-love. Here are some tips:

- **Set clear boundaries.** It can be hard to be assertive with your parents, especially when they are so controlling of everything you do. However, eventually, you will need to put your foot down and let them know that you will not live your life with the primary goal of pleasing them anymore. If you are still living with your narcissistic parent, it might be safer to do this if you have a place where you can stay for a while, because you don't know your parent will react to this, which brings us to the next tip.

- If you have not moved out yet, **talk to a friend or family member whom you can trust and ask them if you can stay with them for a while** in case your narcissistic mother or father lashes out at you when you try to confront them. Don't do anything crazy before you have this reassurance, or you might end up on the streets.

- **Acknowledge the enabling parent** and deal with the feelings you have toward them as well. For each narcissistic parent, there is an enabling one. This means that the other parent is aware of what is happening to you but never tries to defend you. Although this is not direct abuse, it is perfectly normal to feel some resentment toward them also. Those are also emotions that you need to explore and become at peace with so that you don't let them be bottled up inside of you.

How to Heal from Growing up with a Narcissistic Parent

Whichever one of the three situations we described in

the first paragraph of the section above is yours, there is something you still need, and that is healing. Being raised by a narcissistic parent does not make for an easy childhood, and it has most likely left some wounds that you may not have dealt with yet.

- **Allow yourself to grieve the childhood and the loving parents you never had.** It is impossible to go back in time, so you will never have the childhood that you deserved. That is a hurtful thought but one you must deal with. By grieving what you did not have, you can more easily come to terms with it and move to greater things.

- **Focus on building your self-esteem.** When you were a kid, you were never the focus. Once you free yourself from your narcissistic parent, that is something that needs to change. You probably will not be able to see your self-worth in the beginning, and that is why this is a continuous process. You will have to learn something you have never done, which is doing things for yourself and your own happiness. It might feel wrong at first because it is so distant from the reality you have lived for so many years, but with time, it becomes natural. Once again, talking to a therapist or going to a support group can be helpful.

- **Reflect on your past and confront what happened to you.** Doing this exercise will help you accept your life experiences up to that point, and accepting is a very important part of recovering. You can do this by yourself by meditating or writing—for example, with a loved one by opening up or with a therapist who will know how to guide you through the memories.

- **Pursue healthier relationships.** Sometimes, children of a narcissist are so used to that kind of toxic connection that they end up trying to find it in their other relationships, be it romantic or friendships. Break the cycle by actively looking for people who are far away from being narcissistic. Internalize that you deserve true love and affection, and don't settle for anything less!

Healing from Narcissistic Parenting: Sonia's Example

The example I gave on chapter 3 was the one of Sonia, a daughter of a narcissistic father and an enabling mother. Her father had always tried to turn her into the football player he never was. When she left home, she was dealing with severe mental illness because of the trauma she had endured.

She knew she had to heal from it, so she started going to therapy with the support of her good friend Tania. Recovery was a lengthy process, but with the help of the doctor, she was able to come to terms with her childhood by doing exercises that allowed her to reflect on what she had experience and focus on the good things that were going to come from then on.

Having the support of her friend Tania, a very altruist, loving person, was key to Sonia's healing process because she realized that even though she did not get the love that she deserved from her parents, that did not mean that she was not worthy of it or that there were not people out there capable of honestly loving her.

With Your Narcissistic Sibling

Just like with parents, growing up with a narcissistic brother or sister is particularly hard because they are family and it is hard to escape from family when you are young, as toxic as your relationships may be. Here are some things you can do to prevent them from manipulating you and hurting you deeply:

- **Don't share too much information about your life** with them, especially sensitive information. As mentioned before, your narcissistic sibling will take anything they can use against you, so make an effort not to feed that habit of theirs. If you have a partner, talk to them and tell them to do the same.

- **Remember that there is always the family you choose: your friends.** It can be heartbreaking to have a sibling who is not the confidant that you were expecting them to be. But some friendships become so intense that the person becomes like your brother from another mother or your sister from another mister.

- Learn how to **agree to disagree**. Some fights will not be worth fighting, and as much as you want your sibling to see that they are not right, insisting and turning into a heated conversation will probably only do more harm than good. Remember that your sibling will see you trying to prove your point as you are attacking their superiority, so if it is an unimportant matter, be the bigger person (which, let's be real, is not hard when dealing with a narcissist) and learn to let it go.

Parenting a Narcissistic Child

This situation is a bit different because there are two reasons why your son or daughter might be a narcissist in the making: biological ones and environmental ones. The first ones you can't do much about, but the second one relates to the way you and your partner are raising the child. So you will need to analyze what you are doing and understand, from that, what could be causing the kid to showcase narcissistic traits.

A few common habits that parents have and that tend to culminate in the development of a narcissistic personality on their children are the following:

- **Not telling them off when they do something bad.** Your child needs to grow up understanding the difference between good and bad, and it is your job to teach them so.

- **Praising them for no reason.** It is important to congratulate your child when they do good so that they grow up feeling appreciated and with a healthy sense of self-worth. However, constantly applauding them, even when there is no reason to, will only make them feel like they are perfect and create an unrealistic image of themselves and their skills.

- **Being the abusive or the enabling parent.** Children of abusive narcissists can turn into narcissists themselves. Because they are not getting the love and support that they need to develop in a healthy way, they end up believing that they can only depend on themselves as they grow up, and that can create an egoistic personality.

Tips to Deal with a Narcissist Friend

Friends are supposed to be people you can have fun with and you can confide in, not people who talk trash about everyone and expect you to be there for them 24/7 while showing no support or interest in your life. So what can you do when someone in your group of friends fits in the second category?

- Have a conversation with them about their behavior but with a specific approach by **telling them how certain things they do are damaging their reputation**. Make it about them because that is the language they understand the best. Maybe by becoming aware of how their actions are affecting the way others see them, they will think twice before doing certain things.

- **If it comes to that, stop hanging out with them.** What is the point in spending time with someone you don't feel comfortable with and does not even try to have a good time with you anymore? After a while, it becomes nothing but energy consuming for you and the rest of the group, and as difficult as it might be to accept because you became friends with that person for a reason, it comes to a point where there is not much you can do to change their demeanor.

Dealing with a Narcissistic Friend: Paul's Example

Paul's narcissistic friend was Marc, a guy he met at the dog park whom he really clicked with at first. After a while, Marc started demanding too much time and attention from Paul and became jealous of anyone that Paul hanged out with. Paul got tired of this type of behavior and decided to try to talk to Marc, telling him that his other friends thought that the way he acted was not cool at all and that was making him reconsider their friendship. Marc was really offended at first but passive-aggressively told Paul that he would back off, which he did, but not for long. Paul could not take such an energy-consuming friendship anymore and, after a while, decided it was best for him to cut ties with Marc. It was too much and completely unfair to Paul, and in the end, after one attempt to make things better, it just did not seem to be a friendship worth finding for.

Tips to Deal with a Narcissist at Work

If It Is Your Coworker

- Narcissists don't deal well with critique and feedback, but it is necessary, especially in the workplace. To avoid drama, when you need to give your coworker some not so positive feedback, **use the sandwich approach**. This means that you start with something positive, then slip in the feedback, and end on a positive note.

- If they have stolen ideas from you before, **try to**

have proof that said ideas actually came from you. For example, if you already have something in mind before the brainstorming sessions, take notes on your computer and save them. If it comes to that, you can show that you wrote it down before you and the coworker even talked about it since the computer saves the exact date and time that you created the document. This might seem petty, but sometimes you need to be that way if you don't want the narcissist to win.

Dealing with a Narcissistic Coworker: Susie's Example

Susie, a young woman who had always dreamed of becoming a photographer, had seen her dreams become a reality when she started working for a photography agency. Everything was going great until Brock, an egoistic, self-absorbed man, became her coworker. Brock had the habit of taking credit for Susie's ideas, so after several failed attempts at speaking with him and making him realize that they had to split the credit if they were to work together as a team, she decided to do a brainstorming session of her own, creating a document on her computer with several general ideas. She did not lose much time on it as she had other things to do and did not want to compromise those tasks because of Brock—he was doing enough damage already.

When they go talk with their boss with the ideas, Brock does the usual and steals Susie's idea. Susie does not say anything right away as by now she already knows how unpredictable Brock's reactions can be. Once the meeting is over, she asked their boss if they can speak privately. She explains what has been going on and shows the boss the document she created and the time at which she did. Her boss tells her she will speak to Brock and that she will be present on their next brainstorming session because she wants her company to be fair for everyone.

Susie knows that Brock will not react well to their boss's reprehension, but more importantly, she knows she shed some light on a dishonest situation that was happening that no one noticed before.

If It Is Your Boss

- **Try to understand the things that your boss gives more importance to and be excellent at those.** They probably want everything you do to be absolutely perfect, but some things will likely seem to be more relevant to them. Since it will be practically impossible for you to excel at every single task you do, try to do those specific things the best you can so that you avoid some drama.

- However, **don't let the things you do to avoid drama distract you from your own goals**. Don't forget why you started working there and what you want to achieve in your career.

- **Start actively looking for another job.** As much as you can avoid their narcissistic ways while you work for them, the chances of them changing for one of their employees are very slim. Don't quit until you have been accepted in another company, but know that the best way of dealing with a narcissistic boss is by simply removing yourself from the situation.

Dealing with a Narcissistic Boss: Coby's Example

In Coby's case, which was mentioned earlier in the book, his boss had ruined his dream of being a creative copywriter by abusing her power and showing no appreciation for his good work. By the end, when she was confronted by him on her demeanor, she told him he was fired once his internship was over, so he started looking for a job right away.

During the time he had left, he worked as hard as he could on the things that he knew she cared about while also working to build his portfolio and impress any agency he applied for. He stopped working more than the stipulated eight hours a day so that he was not as tired all the time, but he tried to enjoy and learn as much as he could, which would then benefit him in his next professional adventure. In the end, his boss would be the one losing the most.

Step 5: A Summary

1. Is your boyfriend or girlfriend the narcissist in your life? **If they are abusive in any way toward you**, you need to talk to a loved one about your situation for support and **leave as soon as you get the chance to**. However, **if they honestly want to change** and have asked you for your help, you need to, firstly, think if you are willing to do that for someone who has probably hurt you before or not. If you are, **set your boundaries** and be firm about them, and **be open to understanding** where their narcissism is coming from and how you can help them fight it.

2. Is the narcissist in your life a family member? If it is one of your parents or siblings, find ways of dealing with them without triggering them too much but also while making sure you are respected. When you can, remove yourself from the situation and try to surround yourself with people who are more altruistic and loving. And most importantly, work toward **healing from the childhood you experienced and accepting that the best is yet to come**.

3. However, if the narcissist (in the making) is your son and daughter, **analyze the way you and your partner are raising them and what you can change to eliminate the egoistic tendencies of your child**.

4. In case the narcissism comes from one of your friends, **try to start a conversation about their behavior** but in a language that will not offend them easily. If they don't show any will to change, distance yourself from them and focus on healthy friendships.

5. Finally, if the narcissist you know is someone in your workplace, **try to find ways to prove that your job is being jeopardized by someone who is dishonest** and cruel, and **never let the negative experience damage the passion** you have for your career. Remember that you can always start looking for another place to work that, so if it comes to that, the narcissist will lose a valuable team member while you will most likely start a more exciting, happy phase of your career and life.

Conclusion

We all know someone who is a little bit full of themselves. That is not always a bad thing; sometimes it can even be funny. But when it turns into something that damages lives, it becomes something that needs to be addressed.

If you believe you have a narcissistic personality disorder, the best thing you can do is book an appointment with a therapist. A professional will be able to diagnose and help you better than anyone. Besides that, you will need to come clean and be honest with those whom you have hurt so that they can understand where you were coming from and, hopefully, be open to fixing the relationship. Recovery is a lengthy process that requires a lot of hard work and willpower, but you know deep down that, in the end, it is absolutely worth it.

If, on the contrary, you suspect someone you know suffers from the personality disorder, remember to put yourself first before you even think about helping them. Know that you cannot help someone if they don't want to work toward getting better and that you don't owe them anything even if they try to convince you that you do. If the narcissist you know seems to be truly invested in getting better and you decide that you want to help, set your boundaries, but try to understand them, their past, and what led to the development of the condition, as well as what triggers their narcissistic rage and how you can help them manage their emotions.

Narcissistic personality disorder is a serious condition but one that can be overcome as long as the desire and motivation are there.

100% FREE Ebook!

LEARN HOW YOU CAN ENJOY YOUR GADGETS WITHOUT LOSING YOUR ABILITY TO COMMUNICATE IN REAL LIFE!

Claim Your Free Copy Now!
https://maxjharrison.com/moderntechnology

Resources

Abby. (n.d.). Vulnerable narcissism: The less obvious narcissist. Retrieved from https://www.thrivetalk.com/vulnerable-narcissism/

Aconsciousrethink.com. (2019, Feb 26). 7 healing affirmations for victims of narcissistic abuse. Retrieved from https://www.aconsciousrethink.com/3949/7-healing-affirmations-victims-narcissistic-abuse/

Ambardar, S. (2018, May 16). Narcissistic personality disorder: Practice essentials, background, pathophysiology and etiology. Retrieved from https://emedicine.medscape.com/article/1519417-overview#a1

Amherst.edu. (2009, Jan 23). Mirror effect. Retrieved from https://www.amherst.edu/media/view/117821/original/Mirror%2BEffect%2B-%2BChapter%2B4.pdf

Annie Wright Psychotherapy. (2018, May 27). How to recover from growing up with a narcissistic parent. Retrieved from https://anniewrightpsychotherapy.com/how-to-recover-from-growing-up-with-a-narcissistic-parent/

Balance Psychologies (2018, Mar 26). The fate of narcissism in old age. Retrieved from https://www.balancepsychologies.com/single-post/2018/03/26/The-Fate-Of-Narcissism-In-Old-Age

Balsis, S., Eaton, N., Cooper, L. & Oltmanns, T. (2011, May 31). The presentation of narcissistic personality disorder in an octogenarian: Converging evidence from multiple sources. Retrieved from https://www.ncbi.nlm.nih.gov/pmc/articles/PMC3104277/

Bash, A. (2017). Narcissistic siblings and the pain you feel from them. Retrieved from https://families.media/narcissistic-siblings-and-the-pain-you-feel-from-them

Behan, C. (n.d.). 10 ways to spot a narcissistic man on a first date. Retrieved from https://www.meetmindful.com/10-ways-to-spot-a-narcissistic-man-on-a-first-date/

Benthamopen.com. (2019). Visual social media use moderates the relationship between initial problematic internet use and later narcissism. Retrieved from https://www.benthamopen.com/ABSTRACT/TOPSYJ-11-163

Bonior, A. (2017, Sep 29). Are narcissists more likely to be abusive? Psychology Today. Retrieved from https://www.psychologytoday.com/us/blog/friendship-20/201709/are-narcissists-more-likely-be-abusive

Borderline Personality Disorder Treatment (n.d.). 4 tips to surviving a relationship with a person with narcissistic personality disorder. Retrieved from https://www.borderlinepersonalitytreatment.com/narcissistic-personality-disorder-relationship.html

Bridges to Recovery. (n.d.). Narcissistic personality disorder treatment. Retrieved from https://www.bridgestorecovery.com/narcissistic-personality-disorder/narcissistic-personality-disorder-treatment/

Burgemeester, A. (n.d.). Some important narcissistic leaders in history. Retrieved from https://thenarcissisticlife.com/some-important-narcissistic-leaders-in-history/

Burgemeester, A. (n.d.). The inverted (mirror) narcissist. Retrieved from https://thenarcissisticlife.com/the-inverted-mirror-narcissist/

Carter, G. & Douglass, M. (2018, Jul 24). The Aging of Narcissus: Just a Myth? Narcissism Moderates the

Age-Loneliness Relationship in Older Age. Retrieved from https://www.ncbi.nlm.nih.gov/pmc/articles/PMC6066667/

Covertnarcissism.com. (n.d.). Overt versus covert. Retrieved from https://www.covertnarcissism.com/overt-versus-covert

D, J. (2017, April 17). Cerebral vs somatic narcissist: What is the difference and how to spot each. Retrieved from https://www.learning-mind.com/cerebral-somatic-narcissist/

Decision-making-confidence.com. (n.d.). Somatic narcissist. Retrieved from https://www.decision-making-confidence.com/somatic-narcissist.html

Degges-White, S. (2018, Feb 8). Narcissistic friends: What's the attraction? Retrieved from https://www.psychologytoday.com/us/blog/lifetime-connections/201802/narcissistic-friends-what-s-the-attraction

Depression Alliance. (n.d.). Avoidant attachment: The advanced guide. Retrieved from https://www.depressionalliance.org/avoidant-attachment/

Depression Alliance. (n.d.). Vulnerable narcissism: A step-by-step guide. Retrieved from https://www.depressionalliance.org/vulnerable-narcissism/

Dodgson, L. (2018, Oct 22). How to leave a narcissist in 14 steps. Retrieved from https://www.thisisinsider.com/how-to-leave-a-narcissist-in-14-steps-2018-10

Ekern, J. (2013, April 15). Narcissistic personality disorder treatment. Retrieved from https://www.addictionhope.com/mood-disorder/narcissistic-personality/treatment/

Erichfromm.net. (n.d.). Erich Fromm. Retrieved from http://www.erichfromm.net/

Evans, M. (2016, Feb 19). A deeper look at idolise, devalue, discard: The 3 phases of narcissistic abuse. Retrieved from https://blog.melanietoniaevans.com/idolise-devalue-discard-the-3-phases-of-narcissistic-abuse-part-1/

Femenia, N. (2018, Aug 29). My husband's a narcissist: Top 10 ways to deal. Retrieved from https://www.yourtango.com/experts/nora-femenia-ph-d/top-10-tips-deal-narcissistic-husband

Foley, M. (2016, July 12). 4 signs you may be a vulnerable narcissist. Retrieved from https://www.bustle.com/articles/172220-4-signs-you-may-be-a-vulnerable-narcissist

Forbes. (2018, Jan 18). How to handle a narcissist boss according to a psychotherapist. Retrieved from https://www.forbes.com/sites/quora/2018/01/18/how-to-handle-a-narcissist-boss-according-to-a-psychotherapist/#4140ee89158e

Freeman, R. (2017, Feb 22). How to tell you're dealing with a malignant narcissist. Retrieved from https://www.psychologytoday.com/us/blog/neurosagacity/201702/how-tell-youre-dealing-malignant-narcissist

Ghazal, R. (2016, Oct 19). Which countries show the most empathy and who comes last? Retrieved from https://www.thenational.ae/opinion/which-countries-show-the-most-empathy-and-who-comes-last-1.196873

Greenberg, E. (2017, May 28). How do children become narcissists? Retrieved from https://www.psychologytoday.com/intl/blog/understanding-narcissism/201705/how-do-children-become-narcissists

Greenberg, E. (2018, Feb 17). 7 steps to changing your narcissistic responses. Retrieved from https://www.psychologytoday.com/us/blog/understanding-narcissism/201802/7-steps-changing-your-narcissistic-responses

Greenberg, E. (2019, April 6). Is couples' therapy useful when one partner is a narcissist? Retrieved from https://www.psychologytoday.com/intl/blog/understanding-narcissism/201904/is-couples-therapy-useful-when-one-partner-is-narcissist

Gregory, C. (2019, Feb 5). What to Do About Narcissistic Personality Disorder? Retrieved from https://www.psycom.net/personality-disorders/narcissistic/

Grey, S. (2013, Feb 28). The three phases of a narcissistic relationship cycle: Overevaluation, devaluation, discard. Retrieved from https://esteemology.com/the-three-phases-of-a-narcissistic-relationship-cycle-over-evaluation-devaluation-discard/

Hall, J. (2017, April 16). Raised by a narcissist? 11 healing things to do for yourself right now. Retrieved from https://www.huffpost.com/entry/raised-by-a-narcissist-11-healing-things-to-do-for_b_58f2f864e4b0156697722502e

Hammond, C. (2017, Jul 8). Is my child a narcissist. Retrieved from https://pro.psychcentral.com/exhausted-woman/2016/12/is-my-child-a-narcissist/

Hammond, C. (2017, Oct 9). The secret façade of the vulnerable narcissist. Retrieved from https://pro.psychcentral.com/exhausted-woman/2016/11/the-secret-facade-of-the-vulnerable-narcissist/

Happe, M. (n.d.). The relationship between narcissism and codependency. Retrieved from https://www.mentalhelp.net/blogs/the-relationship-between-narcissism-and-codependency/

Health Direct. (2018, Dec). Causes of narcissistic personality disorder (NPD). Retrieved from https://www.healthdirect.gov.au/causes-of-npd

Healthy Place. (2016, July 8). The double reflection narcissistic couples and narcissistic types. Retrieved from https://www.healthyplace.com/personality-disorders/malignant-self-love/the-double-reflection-narcissistic-couples-and-narcissistic-types

Holgate, M. (2017, Nov 30). Are you in a relationship with a narcissist? Retrieved from https://thriveglobal.com/stories/four-stages-of-a-relationship-with-a-narcissist/

Holgate, M. (n.d.). 4 phases of a relationship with a narcissist. Retrieved from https://www.meganholgate.com/2017/05/10/4-phases-of-a-relationship-with-a-narcissist/

Keating, J. (n.d.). How to stop being a narcissist and using people that love you. Retrieved from https://www.lovepanky.com/my-life/better-life/how-to-stop-being-a-narcissist

Krassenstein, E. (2019, Jan 30). Renowned psychologist: Like Hitler, Trump suffers from sadism, malignant narcissism & paranoia. Retrieved from https://hillreporter.com/renowned-phycologist-like-hitler-trump-suffers-from-sadism-malignant-narcissism-paranoia-22815

Kvarnstrom, E. (2016, Jan 8). A one-sided rivalry: The traumatic effects of narcissistic personality disorder on siblings. Retrieved from https://www.bridgestorecovery.com/blog/a-one-sided-rivalry-the-traumatic-effects-of-narcissistic-personality-disorder-on-siblings/

Langley, T. (2016, June 20). Naming evil: Dark triad, tetrad, malignant narcissism. Retrieved from https://www.psychologytoday.com/us/blog/beyond-heroes-and-villains/201606/naming-evil-dark-triad-tetrad-malignant-narcissism

Maccoby, M. (2004, Jan). Narcissistic leaders: The incredible pros, the inevitable cons. Retrieved from https://hbr.org/2004/01/narcissistic-leaders-the-incredible-pros-the-inevitable-cons

Malkin, C. (2016, Sep 30). 8 common, long-lasting effects of narcissistic parenting. Retrieved from https://psychologytoday.com/us/blog/romance-redux/201609/8-common-long-lasting-effects-narcissistic-parenting

Marx, P. (2018, Oct 24). Elon Musk's Twitter meltdowns are symptoms of a much bigger problem for Tesla. Retrieved from https://www.nbcnews.com/think/opinion/elon-musk-s-twitter-meltdowns-are-symptoms-much-bigger-problem-ncna923611

Mayo Clinic. (2017, Nov 18). Narcissistic personality disorder: Symptoms and causes. Retrieved from https://www.mayoclinic.org/diseases-conditions/narcissistic-personality-disorder/symptoms-causes/syc-20366662

McBride, K. (2011, May 1). The narcissistic family tree. Retrieved from https://www.psychologytoday.com/intl/blog/the-legacy-distorted-love/201105/the-narcissistic-family-tree

Meyers, M. (2018, Sep 29). 7 questions to ask when determining whether your partner is a narcissist or just self-absorbed. Retrieved from https://pairedlife.com/problems/Are-You-Dating-a-Narcissist-7-Questions-to-Ask-Yourself-Before-Slapping-That-Over-Used-Label-on-Them

Meyers, S. (2014, Apr 17). I love a narcissist: Now what? Retrieved from https://www.psychologytoday.com/us/blog/insight-is-2020/201404/i-love-narcissist-now-what

Meyers, S. (2014, May 1). Narcissistic parents' psychological effect on their children. Retrieved from https://www.psychologytoday.com/us/blog/insight-is-2020/201405/narcissistic-parents-psychological-effect-their-children

Meyers, S. (2017, Jan 8). The true roots of narcissism. Retrieved from https://www.psychologytoday.com/us/blog/insight-is-2020/201701/the-true-roots-narcissism

Milstead, K. (2018, Mar 12). 8 types of narcissists including one to stay away from at all costs. Retrieved from https://mindcology.com/narcissist/8-types-narcissists-including-one-stay-away-costs/

Ncbi.nlm.nih.gov. (2019, Feb 7). Pathological narcissism: A study of burden on partners and family. Retrieved from https://www.ncbi.nlm.nih.gov/pubmed/30730784

Neuharth, D. (2017, Dec 20). How to deal with a narcissist during the holidays. Retrieved from https://www.yourtango.com/experts/drdanneuharth/deal-narcissist-family-during-holidays

Ni, P. (2014, Oct 12). 6 keys for narcissists to change toward the higher self. Retrieved from https://www.psychologytoday.com/us/blog/communication-success/201410/6-keys-narcissists-change-toward-the-higher-self

Ni, P. (2015, Aug 26). 10 signs your coworker/colleague is a narcissist. Retrieved from https://www.psychologytoday.com/intl/blog/communication-success/201504/10-signs-your-co-worker-colleague-is-narcissist

Ni, P. (2015, Mar 3). 10 signs your boss/manager is a narcissist. Retrieved from https://www.psychologytoday.com/intl/blog/communication-success/201505/10-signs-your-boss-manager-is-narcissist

Ni, P. (2016, Jan 10). 7 signs of a covert introvert narcissist. Retrieved from https://www.psychologytoday.com/us/blog/communication-success/201601/7-signs-covert-introvert-narcissist

Ni, P. (2017, Apr 23). 8 life setbacks and failures of narcissists. Retrieved from https://www.psychologytoday.com/us/blog/communication-success/201704/8-life-setbacks-and-failures-narcissists

Orlando, C. (n.d.). How to spot a narcissist from the first date: Relationship and love advice. Retrieved from https://theproblemismen.com/rants/narcissist

Padovan C. (2017, Dec). The medical-psychiatric origins of the psychoanalytic concept of narcissism. Retrieved from http://www.scielo.br/scielo.php?script=sci_arttext&pid=S1516-14982017000300634&lng=en&nrm=iso&tlng=en

Phatak, R. (2018, Mar 26). Overt vs. covert narcissism: A quick comparison. Retrieved from https://psychologenie.com/overt-vs-covert-narcissism

Pierre, J. (2016, Jul 8). The narcissism epidemic and what we can do about it. Retrieved from https://www.psychologytoday.com/us/blog/psych-unseen/201607/the-narcissism-epidemic-and-what-we-can-do-about-it

Power, C. (n.d.). 5 signs your boss is a narcissist. Retrieved from https://www.mindbodygreen.com/0-16562/5-signs-your-boss-is-a-narcissist.html

Psi.uba.ar. (2012). dsm.pdf. Retrieved from http://www.psi.uba.ar/academica/carrerasdegrado/psicologia/sitios_catedras/practicas_profesionales/820_clinica_tr_personalidad_psicosis/material/dsm.pdf

Psychologia.co. (n.d.). 5 signs they are a somatic narcissist. Retrieved from https://psychologia.co/somatic-narcissist/

Psychology Today. (n.d.). Narcissistic personality disorder. Retrieved from https://www.psychologytoday.com/us/conditions/narcissistic-personality-disorder

Psycom.net. (2018, Nov 25). Free narcissistic personality disorder test. Retrieved from https://www.psycom.net/narcissistic-personality-disorder-test

Ronningstam, E. & Baskin-Sommers, A. (2013, Jun 15). Fear and decision-making in narcissistic personality disorder—a link between psychoanalysis and neuroscience. Retrieved from https://www.ncbi.nlm.nih.gov/pmc/articles/PMC3811090/

Saeed, K. (n.d.). The cerebral narcissist: A portrait. Retrieved from https://kimsaeed.com/2015/06/05/the-cerebral-narcissist-a-portrait-2/

Sage Pub. (2008, Oct 2). Leader emergence: The case of the narcissistic leader. Retrieved from https://journals.sagepub.com/doi/abs/10.1177/0146167208324101

Schulze, L., Dziobek, I., Vater, A., Heekeren, H., Bajbouj, M., Renneberg, B., Heuser, I. & Roepke, S. (2013, Oct). Gray matter abnormalities in patients with narcissistic personality disorder. Retrieved from https://www.sciencedirect.com/science/article/pii/S002239561300157X?via%3Dihub

Schwartz, A. (n.d.). The narcissist versus the narcissistic personality disorder. Retrieved from https://www.mentalhelp.net/blogs/the-narcissist-versus-the-narcissistic-personality-disorder/

Segal, J. & Smith, M. (2018, Oct). Anger management. Retrieved from https://www.helpguide.org/articles/relationships-communication/anger-management.htm/

Skills You Need. (n.d.). Anger management: Self-management techniques. Retrieved from https://www.skillsyouneed.com/ps/anger-management.html

Skodol, A. (2018, Aug). Narcissistic personality disorder (NPD): Mental health disorders. Retrieved from https://www.msdmanuals.com/en-pt/home/mental-health-disorders/personality-disorders/narcissistic-personality-disorder-npd

The Little Shaman. (2019, Jan 29). The narcissistic spectrum. Retrieved from https://pairedlife.com/problems/The-Narcissistic-Spectrum

Thorpe, J. (2016, Dec 2). The 2 main types of narcissism and how to spot the difference. Retrieved from https://www.bustle.com/articles/198007-the-2-main-types-of-narcissism-and-how-to-spot-the-difference

V, A. (2018, Aug 15). What is an inverted narcissist and 7 traits that describe their behavior. Retrieved from https://www.learning-mind.com/inverted-narcissist/

Vaknin, S. (2018, July 2). Dr. Jackal and Mr. Hide (somatic vs. cerebral narcissists). Retrieved from https://www.healthyplace.com/personality-disorders/malignant-self-love/dr-jackal-and-mr-hide-somatic-vs-cerebral-narcissists

Vaknin, S. (2018, July 4). The inverted narcissist. Retrieved from https://www.healthyplace.com/personality-disorders/malignant-self-love/the-inverted-narcissist

Villines, Z. (2018, Aug 7). Codependency and narcissism may have more in common than you think. Retrieved from https://www.goodtherapy.org/blog/codependency-narcissism-may-have-more-in-common-than-you-think-0807187

Webber, R. (2016, Sep 5). Meet the real narcissists (they're not what you think). Retrieved from https://www.psychologytoday.com/us/articles/201609/meet-the-real-narcissists-theyre-not-what-you-think

Wong, B. (2018, July 4). 6 glaring signs your friend is a narcissist. Retrieved from https://www.huffpost.com/entry/signs-your-friend-is-a-narcissist_n_5b311e0ae4b00295f15f716e

Zeiders, C. (2016). Charles Zeiders: A psychoanalytical autopsy of a malignant narcissist in church leadership. Retrieved from https://s3.amazonaws.com/amo_hub_content/Association392/files/2018%20IC/Handouts/Charles%20Zeiders%20-%20A%20Psychological%20Autopsy%20of%20a%20Malignant%20Narcissist%20in%20Church%20Leadership.pdf

www.ingramcontent.com/pod-product-compliance
Lightning Source LLC
Chambersburg PA
CBHW021815170526
45157CB00007B/2602